NURTURE YOUR CHILD'S EMOTIONAL INTELLIGENCE

WELBECK
BALANCE

ABOUT THE AUTHOR

Dr Anne Lane is a clinical psychologist and family therapist. For more than 20 years she has worked in mental health – within both the NHS and her own private practice. Dr Lane has taught on clinical psychology doctorate programmes and run countless workshops on mental health, parenting and emotional regulation. She is a lively, passionate communicator who cares deeply about the lives of the adults, families and children she works with. Anne lives in Hertfordshire, UK, with her husband and three children. For more information, visit her website at www.annelane.co.uk.

NURTURE YOUR CHILD'S EMOTIONAL INTELLIGENCE

5 Steps to Help Your Child
Cope with Big Emotions and
Build Emotional Resilience

BY DR ANNE LANE

WELBECK
BALANCE

A Trigger Book
Published by Welbeck Balance
An imprint of Welbeck Publishing Group
20 Mortimer Street
London W1T 3JW

First published by Welbeck Balance in 2022

Copyright © Anne Lane, 2022

Anne Lane has asserted her right under the Copyright, Designs and Patents Act, 1988, to be identified as the Author of this work.

All rights reserved. No part of this publication may be reproduced, stored in a retrieval system, or transmitted in any form or by any means, electronically, mechanical, photocopying, recording or otherwise, without the prior permission of the copyright owners and the publishers.

A CIP catalogue record for this book is available from the British Library

ISBN
Trade Paperback – 978-1-78956-262-0

Typeset by Lapiz Digital Services
Printed in Great Britain by CPI Group (UK) Ltd, Croydon CRO 4YY

10 9 8 7 6 5 4 3 2 1

Note/Disclaimer

Welbeck Balance encourages diversity and different viewpoints. However, all views, thoughts, and opinions expressed in this book are the author's own and are not necessarily representative of Welbeck Publishing Group as an organization. All material in this book is set out in good faith for general guidance; no liability can be accepted for loss or expense incurred in following the information given. In particular, this book is not intended to replace expert medical or psychiatric advice. It is intended for informational purposes only and for your own personal use and guidance. It is not intended to diagnose, treat or act as a substitute for professional medical advice. Professional advice should be sought if desired before embarking on any health-related programme.

www.welbeckpublishing.com

CONTENTS

PROLOGUE

When I was a child, I found the emotions surrounding me very confusing. Like most children I was happy with the agreeable, enthusiastic emotions. The ones that arrived when fun or exciting things were underway and when I felt loved and encouraged. They felt warm and safe. They were full of energy and possibility.

I was also keen on the proud emotions that popped up when the things I did met with praise and support. When these emotions were around, things seemed clear and busy and righteous. The proud emotions were incredibly good at keeping uncertainty and worry at bay.

Although these emotions were very welcome, there were many other emotions that were less wanted. My least favourite emotions were the difficult and intense ones that created panic and urgency. These emotions seemed to push me to behave in ways that were tricky to explain. Even worse, they made my parents worry and this always left me feeling ashamed and confused. I wished I could get rid of these difficult emotions forever, but however hard I tried to push them away, they bounced back forcefully.

There were also the emotions that I had very little awareness of, but which nudged my behaviour daily. The emotions behind my need to tell an outrageously untrue story, the emotions that led to me avoiding unusual foods, the emotions that made me unkind to friends. I might look back at these behaviours but could not quite be sure why they happened.

Although emotions can feel tiring, overwhelming, confusing, sometimes even painful for your child, they have a purpose. They have the potential to give her life value and direction. They help communicate, problem solve and respond creatively and dynamically. They help her relate to others; they are what makes her human.

Yet, as your child grows up, learning about these emotions can be somewhat ad hoc and confusing. Sometimes they create pleasure in those around her. At other times, alarm and panic. She hears them talked about as though they can be turned *on* or *off* like working levers on a sophisticated drinks machine ('*Today I want there to be less boredom, more happiness, less worry, more appreciation*').

Unfortunately, rather than easing difficult emotions and opening up quieter, more settled feelings, the reactions and directions your child experiences from those around her can increase feelings of confusion and overwhelm. Her emotions become jumpy and erratic and more difficult to deal with, and her confidence in these emotions dwindles. She comes to believe that some emotions are acceptable and some need to be hidden or pushed away. She doubts her own experiences and preferences.

At a time when there is so much worry about children's mental health it's important that children are clearly able to understand and communicate their experiences; that emotions are spoken about and responded to in a way that makes sense to children and that helps them to feel secure and comfortable and safe.

INTRODUCTION

Emotional Intelligence and Your Growing Child

To get through life, a child needs to develop a whole range of skills and understandings. As a parent you take this seriously. You teach her how to dress, how to read, how to write. You explain the weather and rainbows, why people have jobs and why refusing to wash is a bad idea. But when it comes to explaining the intense, forceful, baffling emotions that accompany your child through her days, well, this part of parenting can feel difficult and vague.

A PARENT'S HEARTFELT CONNECTION

As a parent, watching your child's emotions can be very tough. It's hard to know how to help. You see your child struggle, caught up in, and often distressed by, a whirr of emotions that she doesn't understand. Author and journalist Elizabeth Stone famously said: *'Making the decision to have a child is momentous. It is to decide forever to have your heart go walking around outside your body.'* The heartfelt connection you feel toward your child is the thing that drives you forward. It pulls you out of bed at 3am in the morning when she cries, it hooks in your attention as she toddles around the playground or tries to make new friends.

As she gets older, this strong connection pushes you to check that she has brushed her teeth properly and learnt her spellings. But this same binding care, when related to emotions, can become a heavy load. Sometimes in your great attention to detail, you begin to feel that you are responsible for shaping and creating your child's emotions. Not just for ensuring that she's safe and secure, but rather trying to make sure that she's happy and interested and having fun.

When you experience this, the weight of these emotions becomes almost unbearable, particularly when you notice her feeling unsettled or struggling. You want to make the difficult, upsetting emotions she is experiencing go away, but it isn't that simple. You begin to feel frustrated, worried, and then ashamed and guilty.

My aim throughout this book is to help simplify and ease the process of learning about and supporting your child's emotions. I want to help you understand your role and put to rest the unhelpful ideas around emotions that can make a parent's load so hard.

A focus on emotional intelligence will allow you to see how your child's emotions shift and vary. When you realize that you can't make emotions go away or somehow magically summon 'better emotions', you are able to *stay with* your child's experiences and bring her back to connection and understanding. You come to understand that her big or fearful emotions don't necessarily mean big or deep problems, rather they can mean that a child is temporarily struggling and needs your help to calm and slow things down.

Supporting a child's emotional intelligence is not about trying to smooth over her emotions, or helping her to become more polite or extrovert or popular or successful. It's helping her to be real. Being real means feeling worried and sad and vulnerable but also experiencing connection and curiosity and passion. Making mistakes but noticing, listening and learning from them. It's about her finding a place in the world, learning how to be with others and discovering what she thinks, values and wants.

WHAT IS EMOTIONAL INTELLIGENCE?

When we think about how children establish the skills of emotional intelligence – also referred to as EQ – the two most important 'foundational' skills are *emotion awareness* and *emotion regulation*.

EMOTIONAL AWARENESS

Emotional awareness is essential for your child's emotional development. It is her ability to recognize and then reflect on her emotions, to make sense of these and to decide how she will respond. This awareness is very different to the instinctive reactions she had as a young child, when her reactions were direct, unfiltered responses without understanding or awareness.

A child's emotional awareness begins when you help her to pause and recognize emotions as things she can know about and gradually influence. In this book I take you through five key steps that will help you to frame these experiences with your child. I show you how to allow her to notice and balance out different emotions, responding from a place of confidence and choice.

REGULATING EMOTIONS

For a child, regulating emotions means having the ability to manage fast, loud, demanding or fearful emotions so that she can get on with the things of value in her life (for example, building relationships, learning and playing, and growing in independence).

This process starts when she is a young child, during those times when she feels upset or agitated, tired or over-stimulated. You help sooth her, limiting difficult behaviours and reducing demands. As she grows older and more capable, your role changes and develops.

In this book I show you how to slowly help her to begin regulating more tricky, complicated emotions; how to support her to connect compassionately to her struggles; how she can understand and confront her fears. I look at how you can establish limits to those behaviours which intensify and heighten her emotions and how she can use play to express some of the more difficult feelings that might otherwise become dominant and upsetting.

THE SKILLS THAT FOLLOW

Although I have outlined the two principal skills of emotional intelligence, as you help your child nurture her emotional intelligence, other important skills develop. For example, she gains confidence in her values and is more motivated to pursue these. Her concentration and ability to deal with set-backs improves. She becomes kinder and more patient with herself and others. And she is able to respond openly and easily to others.

With her growing awareness and comfort around emotions, she begins to notice the quieter, more searching emotions that no one seems to talk about. The emotions that nudge at her attention, pushing her to expand her experiences, to make new friends, to develop new skills. She becomes aware of the complicated emotions that hold on to shame or pull her away from others. And whilst she feels vulnerable and wobbly, she slowly learns that she can put her experiences into words, that others will be able to understand and that these emotions will shift.

All of these skills help your child's mental health. They ease distress and increase her sense of connection to others and confidence in herself.

EMOTIONAL INTELLIGENCE AND YOUR CHILD'S MENTAL HEALTH

When we talk about a child's mental health, we're referring to her psychological or emotional health and wellbeing. It is about how she thinks, feels and behaves, how outside events affect her and how well she manages and can reach out to others. When you and your child have a strong understanding of emotional intelligence, her capacity and awareness of her thoughts and feelings become stronger and she is able to seek out your support. In other words, her mental health improves.

Sometimes, a child's emotions become very fearful and unsettled, affecting her thoughts and behaviours and her connection with you. Her mental health suffers, and she struggles to manage age-appropriate demands, such as going to school, maintaining friendships, or having a warm, meaningful family life. Her confidence plummets and the pressure on both her and you can be immense. In these situations, having the support of a compassionate but skilled therapist reduces fear and uncertainty and can help you find a way through, where before things had seemed tight and stuck. Do consider this if you feel it may be appropriate for your child.

ABOUT ME

I am a clinical psychologist. My work has taken me into many different settings – from residential units and schools to outpatient clinics, doctors' surgeries and charities. I see adults, families and children. You'll see many references to my work in these different places throughout this book. There are also a lot of stories from my own young family. I am the mother of three children (currently aged six, eight and ten years old). These three have taken me in hand and, with unbroken energy, have put me through the most rigorous emotional training.

At the heart of all my work is a concern with emotional intelligence. I am not a person who believes that we should be simplistically led by the handful of emotions that are most familiar or shout loudest. Our emotions can be knotty and tangled and confusing. Taken in isolation they can be contradictory and whimsical. Instead, I am very keen to understand and listen to all emotions, and then slowly and gradually work out how best to help a person make use of these emotions so as to pursue a life of deep connection and value.

WHY I WROTE THIS BOOK

My understandings and experiences with emotions have been shaped by two big forces in my life: my clinical training and work, and my life as a mother. I am never sure which to put first, particularly when writing a book about children. Both my work and my family life immersed me in the world of emotions. Particularly the emotions experienced by parents and children.

When I was newly qualified and trying to make sense of therapeutic work, I was in urgent need of approaches that would help me to make sense of the emotions and experiences people and families described. Narrative Therapy brought a hopefulness and irreverence to a world of psychiatry and psychology, full of 'serious' problems, particularly in my work with children and families.

Narrative Therapy engages people in thinking about the stories they tell themselves about their emotions, the problems they experience, their lives and what they value. Narrative Therapy seeks to separate people out from diagnostic labels. A well-known statement from Narrative Therapy is that 'the person is not the problem, the problem is the problem'. You'll notice narrative influences in my work around 'Sneaky Poo' in chapter 6 and in my attention to play in chapter 8. Narrative Therapy felt hopeful and bright-eyed, and it introduced me to a world of possibilities and emotional connection.

One of the problems with some of the therapies taught during my training was that they would 'invent' the ways in which families and children should be feeling. They inevitably focused on trying to manage and adjust thoughts and behaviour to achieve particular emotions, rather than understanding the many emotions, passions and quiet values that were already there.

Acceptance and Commitment Therapy (ACT) brought a slow shift in emphasis. Its attention was on the emotional currents that lie underneath explicit thoughts and obvious behaviours. It highlighted how avoiding or trying to control these emotions would intensify a sense of struggle and difficulty. Understandings from ACT have allowed me to more fully understand the role of acceptance. You'll see the many ways ACT has influenced my work in chapters 2 and 8 particularly.

And then I became a parent, and my need to understand emotions more deeply opened up again. The emotions I felt as a new mother were large and intense. I moved from love to panic, to guilt to panic again. This was when I turned to Donald Winnicott, paediatrician and psychoanalyst. His intelligence and compassion for both parents and children was present in his writings on the 'Good Enough' parent. He helped me to be kind to myself and my children, in the midst of all of these struggles. He made sense of my difficulties and allowed for my imperfections. He knew that my Good Enough was in fact just right for the job and he gave me permission to be more human and real. In chapter 4 I talk about how the idea of Good Enough can be brought into your relationship with your child and how essential it is for her emotional intelligence (and your sanity).

But the real influences on my approach have been the many people and families who I have sat with and spoken to over the years, and of course my own family, whose love and influence has been immense. My nature has always been to enjoy working out the things 'not said', the hopes not noticed, the needs not expressed. When working with emotions there are many contradictions, much heartache and lots of struggles. Emotions are fascinating and helpful and obstructive and confused. And they make my work and my connection to others such a joy.

You'll see through this book that these people and their stories are with me always. They've taught more than any writing or lecture or textbook what it's like to be human, to feel many, often contradictory emotions, to make mistakes, to learn from these mistakes, to make more mistakes and to learn more.

ABOUT THIS BOOK

This book is divided into two parts. Part One takes you through the basics of how emotions work: how a child begins understanding and responding emotionally, the ways she might struggle and how you can help her open up and understand her different emotional responses. Importantly, chapter 4 focuses on Good Enough Parenting. Sometimes, focusing on a child's emotional development can mean we lose sight of the most important and influential relationship underpinning this process. From this perspective Good Enough Parenting is not just sufficient, it is essential for a child's emotional development. Good Enough Parenting allows the spaces for a child to develop and gain her own emotional understandings and then the repairs and reconnections to help her slow down and manage when things get tough. Good Enough means we not only allow a child to balance out her need for independence with her need for support, it also means she witnesses parents and carers who attend to their own emotional needs and capacities.

In Part Two I move on to explore five different ways in which your interactions with your child shape her learning and understanding of emotions, and I give you tools to help your child boost her emotional intelligence. These five steps are intended to show you how you can bring ease and enjoyment to your child's emotional world. They are designed to help you feel less unsure and fearful when approaching your child's emotions, and hopefully make parenting around emotions enjoyable and engaging.

Each of the five steps is split into two sections: the first introduces the step, and shows how it relates to emotional intelligence. The second section takes you through some of the core skills relating to that step. These skills are designed to help you:

- Build emotional ease in your relationship with your child
- Support her in developing an awareness of her emotions
- Help her through difficult, fearful emotions, particularly those that are causing her to withdraw or avoid situations
- Simplify and ease worry and anxiety
- Use play to connect emotionally with her and work through misunderstandings or upset
- Settle big, challenging emotions

A NOTE ON AGE RANGES

This book is aimed at children aged from approximately 4 to 11 years.

Although many of the other skills children develop can be put into generalized age ranges (such as cognitive development or physical abilities), emotions and emotional development are far more idiosyncratic and temperamental.

Much of your child's emotional development depends on the experiences she has, how she adjusts and her own unique sensitivities and strengths. Therefore, in general I refer to the many different themes of emotional development and intelligence, only occasionally referring to specific age ranges.

The important thing is that you support your child through these obstacles as best you can using the skills outlined in this book. At times, a specific skill will work well for a six-year-old but not a nine-year-old, not because of age, but simply because of the challenges she is experiencing. The best way forward is to find an ease and see how things unfold.

AUTHOR'S NOTES

Throughout this book I use stories to illustrate ideas and help to make things easier to understand. All of the stories relating to past clients are amalgamations of many people and interactions that I've had over the years. I have changed names, sometimes gender and life situations, and combined different situations to prevent any untrue associations and ensure anonymity.

In order to make this book simpler to read I loosely alternate the use of 'he' or 'she' through the chapters. Of course, I am referring to all children, but this helps to prevent too many complicated sentences and phrases.

I use the acronym EQ occasionally as shorthand for emotional intelligence. The Q comes from the emotional 'quotient' of a person.

This book is aimed at both parents and carers. I use the term 'parent' or 'adult' to refer to the person who has principal responsibility for the child.

YOUR APPROACH MATTERS

I was a fantastic parent before I had children. I remember one of the first families I worked with as a new assistant psychologist some 25 years ago.

I was absorbed in taking one poor father through a complex star chart reward system whilst he tried to manage three children. It was like World War III. 'Yeah... yeah... you're right,' he said patiently as the five-year-old tried to lift the back legs of his chair up. 'Hmm...' he said as the seven-year-old announced that the baby had pooed himself. 'Of course...' he murmured as the buggy crashed down and the milk exploded. 'The trouble is, Anne, that I spend most of my time trying to simply stop them seriously injuring themselves.'

Parenting can be the most mind-boggling job. The demands are endless and there are all of the many invisible emotional minefields when for some reason or other your child won't let you wash banana out of her hair (*'I like it like that!'*), when her teacher calls you in after school to tell you just how concerned she is about your child's behaviour, when your eight-year-old tells you that she will never be able to sleep in her own bed *'ever again'*.

And then that nagging voice enters your head. You think *'But this is my fault. Why can't I manage this? Why do I keep messing up? I'm sure I'm causing all of these problems.'* Your mind returns to the mistakes you've made, the things you could have planned better, the frustration and anger you shouldn't have expressed.

But the truth is that your child brings her own personality, capacity for learning, sensitivity, temperament, difficulty adjusting – just as you do. And each family faces demands and pressures that are unique to them and which no one else can fully understand or know.

And so, a central aim of this book is to help you hold on to a sense of compassion – toward yourself – because you love your child and you are trying hard. I want you to know that not only is it okay and very normal to fail, but that these failures provide all sorts of opportunities for growth and understanding and connection (not to mention greater resilience and an expanded sense of humour).

When you can connect to some of this compassion, you discover what a capable parent you really are. You start to not just love your child, but also to actually enjoy her emotions and the opportunities and challenges they bring.

PART ONE

UNDERSTANDING EMOTIONS

1

YOUR CHILD'S WORLD OF EMOTIONS – AND YOUR ROLE IN IT

Sometimes it seems like your child is one big bundle of emotion. Whatever she is feeling – be it boredom, rage or bitter disappointment – there isn't much of a filter. Her emotions sit very near to the surface, popping up quickly and instinctively.

Trying to understand and help her with these emotions can feel like walking around in the dark, bumping into things. It's hard to work out where they came from, what they might really be about or how you should respond.

In this chapter we'll look at how your child learns about her emotions, from back when she was a young child through to now. And we'll look at your role: how you can connect with her to help her shape her understanding and responses to these emotions, soften and slow down big, fearful emotions and put language to her experiences.

A FLOOD OF EMOTIONS

It was a cold, dark morning. Six-year-old Ned, normally pretty easy going and cheery, was tetchy and cross. He had wet himself in the toilet having just got his school clothes on – and his big brother, Ash, had laughed and called him a baby. Feeling upset and ashamed, Ned pushed Ash and Ash had fallen against a window with no small amount of noise and drama.

Now, alongside the upset of wetting himself, his mum had become cross and told him off.

Then it was breakfast – Ned always enjoyed his toast with honey. As he sat down, his face crumpled. 'This toast is yucky and dusty!' he stated loudly, staring at the crumbs scattered around the plate. 'I hate it. And I have a tummy ache,' he added, putting his head down on the table.

Ned's mum looked over. 'Oh no. That silly toast,' she said as she rubbed his head. 'You are having a tricky morning, aren't you? Poor thing.' Ned's eyes welled up with tears and he pulled at his mum's top so that she crouched down to give him a hug. 'You're my lovely boy,' said his mum as she wrapped her arms around him.

Ned was having a difficult time on that morning. With so many emotions rushing through him he was feeling pushed and pulled around. There were the vulnerable emotions, the defensive emotions, the emotions that wanted it all to be the toast's fault. Then there were the emotions that drew his attention to how nice it would be if his mum could make all of this better and that wondered if having a tummy ache would necessitate this.

All of these emotions were working hard for Ned; busily sorting through events and considering different responses. Some of the emotions were dashing in, some were holding back, others were slowly working up the courage to reach out and connect.

Your child, like Ned, will be continuously trying to figure out the world and sort out her reactions through emotions. Emotions are with her constantly, analysing and responding to various situations.

They could be reacting to her imagination: she thinks about an air adventure team she saw on TV – she feels excited, her hand moves, soaring over a wall then swooping down to push a stone off the edge, before rising into the sky again.

Equally her emotions could be helping her figure out how she responds to the long set of stairs she must climb ahead, assessing her background energy levels, how excited she feels about the warm bath waiting for her, whether it would be better to get her dad to carry her or to avoid the task, and instead play a game darting around her parents' legs.

It's often tempting to think of a child's emotional responses as basic reflexes; easily identifiable and fairly simple. So, a child might feel sadness in response to loss, anger as a reaction to threat and happiness when good things are happening. Whilst this seems to make sense (we all readily link a smiling face to 'happy' or crying to 'sad'), it doesn't do justice to the responsive, agile way in which her emotions can work. The reality is that behind a smile, a frown or a tear are *many* different, complex experiences and understandings. Just as with adults, children are not passive recipients of specific emotional experiences. Instead, they put together their emotional responses using a range of experiences and understandings, creating reactions and ways of adapting that are anything other than simple.

The important thing about these more nuanced and agile emotions is that when they are working well, they are constantly updated and adjusted. They allow a child to pull together lots of different information and to make a 'best guess' at how to interpret and respond. Sometimes they react in ways that are quirky and unexpected. At other times they are heartfelt and honest. But being so agile and responsive, your child's emotions need a lot of kind help and guidance. Unguided and away from an adult's care, a child's emotions can quickly become confused and bewildered. They get stuck and defensive and pull your child around in loops.

This is where you come in. These emotions might confuse you too, but you provide the security and safety to help her to quieten down the panic. Gradually, her emotions settle so that together you can make sense of her experiences.

WHEN EMOTIONS BECOME 'DISORIENTATED'

When a child is well rested and comfortable, when she feels secure and safe, her emotions seem to respond simply and naturally. They act like quiet, unobtrusive background workers, gently assessing the situation and providing small, fine-tuned responses. Her emotions adjust to her energy levels and minor changes in her situation, they point out interesting things, good things, things that she can comfortably focus on. Everything seems to go well.

At other times, as was the case for Ned, a child's emotions can be exhausting, volatile and even scary. Ned felt vulnerable. A lot of pressure was being put on his system and he had no clear help. His emotions were trying to cope. They wanted to keep him safe, to take quick action and to sort out his brother, but they didn't want subtle and they didn't want slow. They wanted obvious, strong and decisive. And decisive meant giving Ash a push.

Unfortunately rather than establishing Ned's strength and superiority, his emotional reactions seemed to make things worse. The shove backfired and the situation was more complicated than it had seemed. Ned was in deeper trouble and felt even more worried. With very little confidence left, his emotions tried to push the problem onto his toast, but this didn't seem to work either. Ned was left feeling despondent and hopeless.

Psychologists often describe confused, powerful emotions such as those experienced by Ned as 'disorientated'. Disorientated emotions are:

- **Inexperienced, vulnerable and overwhelming**. They are the emotions that try to deal with situations at speed, without an adult's support.
- **Fuelled by fear and uncertainty**. They are fast and defensive, they look for quick solutions such as acting powerfully, taking control or trying to avoid situations. The gentler, more open emotions get shoved aside.
- **Likely to escalate difficult situations**. Rather than helping to sort a situation out, these emotional responses just escalate difficulties. For a child, these emotions feel lost and out of control. They push her back into more defensive emotional responses and the cycle repeats.

You might recognize that your child experiences these quick, rash, responsive emotions on a regular basis. To help slow these emotions down and to organize and sort through all the different demands and opportunities, your child needs help. She needs a kind, emotionally sturdy adult who can help her out.

THE ROLE PARENTS PLAY

Although disorientated emotions feel frantic and challenging, they are quickly simplified and guided with the help of an adult. When a child's emotions are 'orientated' and connected to an adult, they have a way of understanding and adapting to new and demanding situations. They become more *intelligent*.

If we go back to Ned, somehow when his mum spoke to him in a soft, kind voice, his emotions very quickly eased. They stopped trying to work things out themselves. They changed from agitated and troubled and instead they slowed down and released their hold. They relaxed.

Ned's emotions were able to do this because he had a safe and trusted relationship with his mum. This trusted connection allowed him to build a bridge between the instinctive emotional reactions he had been experiencing and his mum's more grounded, reflective responses. Psychologists call this trusted connection a 'secure attachment'. The more secure a child's attachment to a parent, the more effectively she can use it to understand, adapt and regulate her emotions. This trusted connection doesn't mean she won't have big, difficult, challenging emotions, but it does mean that she can navigate them more easily.

HOW IS A SECURE ATTACHMENT CREATED?

Children begin developing attachments toward the end of their first year. Your child will have developed a preference for the person she spent the most time with and who was most dependable, easy and warm. She would have come to understand that that person was available and connected and therefore safe to develop a secure attachment when they:

- Listened and responded to her, gazing at her, following her interests and chatting to her easily throughout the day
- Brought her close to them when she was upset, holding her, rocking her, stroking her and talking to her in a soothing, reassuring voice
- Watched and listened to her for cues around her needs, noticing if she seems to be pulling away (and making some space for this) but also noticing when she wants to be closer

- Communicated clearly and evenly, letting her know when something is dangerous or not allowed, but equally comforting her quickly and warmly if she seemed unnerved or anxious

Think back to your child's first year and you will likely recall many moments of connection as described above. These interactions were the foundation for the connection you have now.

It's important to recognize that a parent doesn't have to do these things perfectly. In fact there is no possible way of doing these things perfectly. Rather, the essential thing is that a child's adult is sincere and heartfelt in their efforts and that they persist even when things are difficult. Don't panic if you recall times when you felt you were too busy to give your younger child your full attention, or if things were fraught or difficult.

The truth is that for many parents there are times when your relationship to a child can become strained or hard and your child is less connected than you would want to be. The important thing is that you notice the many opportunities there are to reconnect with her now, as she continues to grow and develop, whilst acknowledging and learning from the past.

CONNECTED EMOTIONS

A secure attachment means that a child trusts that her parent will tune in enough and be responsive enough to help and guide her emotional responses. When a child has a secure attachment to you she spends a lot of time watching your reactions (in preference to other people's) and she uses your emotional understandings and responses as a proxy for her own experience. This emotion bond is strong; with you around, her emotions have a way of making sense of things and sorting out more useful ways of responding.

When a child has a secure attachment to a parent:

- She relies on them to steady her strong, loud emotions; to comfort her fearful emotions; to make sense of emotions that are confused.
- She uses that parent to gain a clearer and more effective way of sorting through all of the different messages and impulses she experiences, both from the outside world and from her own body and nervous system. For example, when someone she doesn't know comes to visit, she watches to see how her adult responds. If her adult doesn't seem comfortable and at ease, she is likely to pick up on that and copy that response.
- She seeks out her adult, trusting that they can somehow understand the meaning of her uncomfortable or unfamiliar feelings (for example, tiredness, overwhelm, sickness or edginess) and work out what to do. She watches to see how they respond. Do they take immediate action? Are they easy and warm, impatient and cross, or curious and open?
- She copies her adult's different emotional responses to see how they feel. You may recall how your child copied your reactions when talking to teddies or dolls or other friends, almost as if they were trying the phrases you used out for size. Over time these 'copies' got adapted and changed. I remember how my son would sooth his teddy just as I soothed him, or my daughter would greet people who came to visit in the same way that I did.

This process can be most intense in a child's first few years (0–4 years), but her relationship to you and access to your emotional responses is central to her emotional learning throughout her childhood. By about four years old, she will have become more familiar with these emotional responses and will have begun changing and adapting them to suit different situations and different demands. In other words, she has developed her own 'reference library' of different emotions which she uses for different settings, adapting and swapping them around. In times of difficulty, she seeks you out again, relying on your guidance and understanding.

PUTTING EMOTIONS INTO LANGUAGE

The emotional connection your child shares with you starts when she is a young baby. Without language to frame things, she watches and learns through your actual physical responses: the tone of your voice, the ease of your gestures, how responsive and tuned in you are. If she is in doubt about something, she looks over to you, checking your reaction. When things feel more unsettling, she comes physically to find you, putting her head onto you, waiting for the feeling to pass.

This non-verbal emotional connection is very effective when she's under four and you or another significant adult[1] are physically available and tuned in to her experiences. Just the way you look or respond is packed full of information and is so efficiently transmitted. You remember a time when your child was upset by a clown at a children's party and you placated her and calmed her, modelling comfort and safety. Her emotions learnt that the situation was safe and that she is safe. They settle.

The problem in those first four years is that you weren't always available. You might have been preoccupied or busy, you might have dropped her at the party. She needed a connection to you that wasn't solely dependent on being physically next to you so that she could become more independent, try out new

---

1 A child normally develops one to two strong, trusted attachments with parents or an important carer and then, ideally a supportive web of secondary attachments with family, close friends, nursery carers, etc.

situations, and even bring 'problems' back to you when she was more ready to think about them.

The best way for her to achieve this was to try to *capture* the emotional experiences for you in language. I saw this with my own daughter when she was about three years old. I had taken her to a soft play area. Whilst we were there, she met a friend and they played for well over an hour. Eventually, the friend went home, and it was time for us to go. Her younger brother was ready for a nap and was beginning to take on a dazed look, but she had just hit over-tired and began to wail. After a bit of a kerfuffle and lots of tears and soothing I finally clipped her into the buggy and we set off home.

When things had calmed down, she asked (as she often did at that age), *'What did I say, Mummy?'*

'Well,' I said, *'you wanted to stay at the soft play and Mummy said, "time to go home" and you were crying.'* She stuck her thumb in her mouth and nodded sagely. The walk home was quite long. Soon something else set off her tears again. After being comforted and soothed she was calm again. She asked, *'What did I say, Mummy?'*

It is difficult to frame questions around emotions and their meaning, even for adults, so I was glad that she had found a way to ask. She had managed *'What did I say?'* when I think she was really wanting to ask *'What was happening to me?'*, *'What was I feeling?'*, *'Why have I been so upset?'*, *'Am I okay?'*

I had another go. I said, *'In the café you were crying and didn't want to leave. I think you're a bit tired and upset.'* She didn't seem to like this and grumbled and muttered so when she asked again, I decided to be gentler and warmer. I tried, *'You were a little bit cry-ey.'* The change in her reaction was marked. *'Yes,'* she said – and added in a soothing voice to herself, *'a bit cry-ey.'*

There is something about emotions that makes them hard to explain or describe.

You'll notice this yourself, a lot of the time they pass by very subtly and you hardly notice their presence. They feel pleasant and supportive. They settle your attention and help you connect to things. At other times they feel frantic and apprehensive. They seem to arrive instantaneously. They hook in your thoughts and behaviours and your wider understanding is left trying to catch up.

For a child, learning to capture these experiences in words – particularly the fast, unsettled emotions – requires a lot of support and practice. Mostly, this happens when her emotions are calmer and more settled, when she feels safe and supported. She will begin this process tentatively as a young child (under four), but this skill really starts to develop with your guidance from 4–11 years.

'WHAT AM I FEELING?'

Having the ability to put her emotions into words is central to the development of emotional intelligence. When a child has this emotional language, she can temporarily hold on to and reflect upon her emotions. She has a way of understanding her experiences, her thoughts, her feelings, her reactions. Whereas before she was just feeling and reacting without perspective, with language she can slow things down and bring the emotion to mind. She can share her experiences with others, she can reflect on her response.

Your child's ability to put words to emotions is a process that shifts and changes as she grows. Although it depends on her language development, it also depends on her access to these types of conversation, how aroused and intense the emotions have been and how quickly they settle. Importantly, it is far easier for a child to speak about her emotions when her attachment to you is secure and settled, when there is a background atmosphere of warmth and acceptance.

On that day with my daughter, her emotions had felt big and urgent. Previously she might have asked to be carried home after such a big outburst: learning through my non-verbal responses that things were safe, but feeling unsure about the earlier dramatic emotions. This time, with her growing ability to talk about things, she was beginning to try to sort her feelings out through language. She needed two things: to make sense of the intense emotions she had experienced, and to know that this experience was safe and generally okay.

At first I had tried offering 'tiredness' and 'upset' to describe her emotions but it was clear these weren't good enough labels. She had been 'tired' before; this time it felt different. Whereas 'upset'? Perhaps upset felt too vague. With 'cry-ey', she knew that we were talking about the right part of her experience. Emotions like to be able to recognize themselves, and this label seemed to allow that. The fact that the emotion could be named meant it was 'a thing'. It could be known about. It could be understood.

Although my daughter was only three years old, this process of trying to understand and name emotions is present in children of all ages and even in adults. As a child becomes school-aged (4–11 years old), she is likely to be less deliberate or open about this process and so it's very helpful if you bear in mind her need to slow down her experiences and find words for her emotions.

When a child is trying to understand her emotions, she instinctively tries to frame her experiences. She wants to know:

- What am I feeling?
- What should I do about this feeling?
- Are my emotions clear and understandable or jumpy and confused?
- How can I put these feelings into words so that someone else can think with me?

This ability to grasp and frame her experiences allows her system to quieten. Her thoughts slow down and focus, she begins recognizing her experiences.

LABELLING EMOTIONS

Giving names or labels to emotions lets your child know that her emotion is a recognizable, knowable experience. She gains confidence that her emotions can be made sense of and shared with others – and so she feels more at ease.

When a child first starts learning to speak, she points to things so that the adults around her can help her to name things. With emotions this is more problematic. They are hidden and they shift and change. I remember my children labelling emotions by pointing to other children. They might soulfully note 'He is very sad' or 'He wants his mummy', but these labels would be mixed in with a range of questions, solutions and of course judgements – 'He is being naughty!'

Discussing the experiences of those around them is a very good way for a child to begin labelling emotions. I would often tell my children how I was feeling: 'I'm a bit worried because I can't find the keys', or 'I am so excited about seeing Aunty Lydia'. I would also use little labels such as, 'Oh that was a surprise', when I saw them react to something unexpected. Or, 'That didn't feel nice' if they had been hurt. Slowly, they would take on my labels. 'I don't feel nice, Mummy,' they might say. Or, 'I am worried about my doll' (copying my statements that I 'worried' about my keys).

Here are some things to bear in mind when you talk to your child about emotions:

- Younger children start labelling emotions with you around. This happens most easily by observing other children or pointing out the feelings of children in stories, etc.

- With big, dynamic emotions, a child will be better able to talk and reflect when these emotions have settled. Starting to talk too quickly can retrigger the emotions so it's best to wait until your child either tries to talk about it herself or after a meal or a nap.
- For children around four years of age you might use either basic emotional terms such as 'happy, cross, sad' or terms linked more to their physical experience of the emotion. For example, 'wobbly inside' to describe an excited state. When the label relates closely to how the emotion physically felt then it helps your child to connect the word with the feeling. This connection is important. Don't worry if the word isn't a 'classic' emotional label. Your child will slowly develop more language and use more commonly recognized labels.
- For four- to seven-year-olds, words that allow more connection are helpful. For example, '*sad, worried, thinky, frustrated*' invite others to enter into reflecting on the emotion compared with the more common 'angry, annoyed, irritated', which are more common but push others away.
- Seven to eleven-year-olds are able to relate to more nuanced labels such as 'embarrassed, nervous, isolated'. If your child is this age, she will also benefit from hearing her emotions described with mixed labels. For example, 'excited-grumpy, nervous-worried, lonely-cross'. This helps her to begin recognizing that there are often a few different emotions present at the same time. It allows her to acknowledge the contradictions in how we can feel and to develop more robust understandings.
- A child will often want you to vary the intensity of a label. Sometimes she wants to turn down a label ('*It wasn't so big*!') and sometimes stress it more ('*I was* really *worried*').

- It can be helpful to give a bit of context to emotion but keep to descriptions rather than evaluations or generalizations as much as possible. You might say, *'You didn't talk much; you asked me to take you home; you didn't want the potatoes,'* rather than *'You wouldn't talk; you demanded I take you home; you never eat'*.
- Take the child's lead, keeping conversations short (a sentence from you; her response; perhaps another sentence from you).
- Use a kind, comfortable tone.

As your child becomes more comfortable talking about her experiences, she can put context to these and understand how she can process these emotions through you. We will go into more detail with this in chapter 3.

PRIORITIZING A CHILD'S EXPERIENCE

One of the most important things when labelling an emotion with your child is to prioritize her experiences and preferences. I mentioned before that the more the child can link the label to her experience, the more she can relax and settle that emotion. This means we offer a label, but we can't know whether that label is going to feel meaningful or connected to her experience, whether it will 'fit'.

It can be very tempting to think we know what a child's emotion means, and to assume that emotions can only be labelled in one way. I remember an old schoolteacher insisting that I was *'lonely'* after my friend had left for a new school. Something about the word didn't fit for me. I preferred it when the dinner lady said, *'Oh your friend going has left you feeling lost.'* Perhaps I felt I could make *'lost'* my own; maybe it sounded kinder. The words used to identify an emotion carry different meanings for different children. The aim is to find words that your child feels connected to.

If the label you offer doesn't seem to fit for your child, then let it go. After you've suggested a label, the best thing to do is to watch and listen. Your child's reaction will let you know whether the label feels helpful. If she is uncomfortable then she might need you to find another word for the emotion, or simply stop and comfort her and perhaps talk about something else.

EMOTIONS ARE OKAY

Although we focus on *naming* the emotion, the child is essentially also learning about the *okayness* of that emotion. A sad emotion named for a child in a gentle, reflective manner is very different from the same sad emotion named in a way that conveys annoyance, shame, uncertainty or dismissal. This is important, because the more comfortable a child feels around an emotion, the more she can reflect on it and make sense of its message.

Sometimes when we are thinking about particular emotions, we carry our own 'baggage' around them. For example, your child's tight, frustrated emotional response might remind you of an unpleasant relationship or past difficulty. You want to close it down and stop it, and this comes over in your body language or tone. It also gets communicated through the way we use labels. For example:

- Using labelling to teach your child 'right' or 'wrong' – '*You don't need to be sad when...*'
- Making the label a description of character – '*You are always so anxious*'

- Giving complicated intentions around a child's emotion – *'You got angry to punish Mummy/You got sad because your sister got more...'*
- Making a child's emotions responsible for yours – *'You're sad and it's making Daddy feel sad!'*

A younger child (aged 4–6 years) needs to learn to communicate her emotions before she can recognize and organize her response. If we try to censor what she says or place judgement around emotions too quickly, she doesn't have the opportunity to increase her awareness or reflect on their meaning. She simply learns that some emotions are 'wrong' or 'bad'.

When an emotion is not 'allowed', a child might become overly hesitant and indirect in her expressions or impulsive and exaggerated in what she says.

When I was a teenager I visited a neighbour's home with my younger siblings. When they announced that they didn't like the cake she gave them, I told them off in a harsh whisper. My sister sat in confused silence looking at the cake on her plate, whilst my brother quietly hid chunks of the cake behind a cushion. If only I had been able to allow for their experience and helped them find a better way of explaining!

When we listen to all a child's emotions and help her open them up, that child begins to also understand how others think about these emotions. She learns to slowly consider other people's feelings whilst also being truthful to her own needs. We will look at how to do this in chapter 3.

POINTS TO REMEMBER

- **Your connection to your child is important**. Your child learns about emotions through you. When she has secure, safe attachment to you she watches to see how you respond to things, learning and copying your reactions.
- **You act as an anchor for difficult fear-based emotions**. A child's limited experiences mean that she often feels uncertain and fearful. In your presence these emotions slow and settle. She learns that these feelings can be managed through you.
- **The way you respond to her emotions matters**. When you respond to her emotions with ease and kindness, she develops an instinctive sense that her emotions – although sometimes fast and difficult to grasp – can be understood, worked through and soothed.
- **Big emotions settle and become less frightening for a child when we name them**. Labelling emotions also helps children to begin putting their experiences into words.
- **Language gives your child a mental map of her emotions**. She can begin to recognize her emotions, how they respond and what she can do about them. When she has words for her emotions she begins to use that emotion to think about her preferences and needs.

2

OPENING UP TO DIFFICULT EMOTIONS

WHEN CHILDREN ARE ABLE TO COMMUNICATE VULNERABILITY

A mum had just returned to work after a gap and was keen to make a good impression. Mornings were very stressful because her four-year-old daughter's nursery was some distance from her son's school and she needed to drop them both off in time to get the train into London. After the usual rush around, the mum managed to somehow get everyone into the car in time. She dropped her son at his school and then parked outside the daughter's morning club. There was a kerfuffle around a water bottle (it had the wrong lid), but a replacement was found. The mum gave her daughter a cuddle and all was fine. She was in good time for the train. As they got out of the car to enter the building, the mum realized her daughter was having difficulty walking. She looked down. The daughter was walking in a pair of her mum's high heels.

The mum felt a weight of defeat and tiredness come down around her as she realized she would miss the train after all. She felt furious. She wanted her daughter to know just how unfair and wrong this was. 'I told her that Mummy would now feel bad when she got to work, that my boss would unfairly judge me, how disappointed and very very sad I was at this behaviour.'

Her daughter's face crumpled. Tears welled up in her eyes. 'Mummy,' she said, 'I am a small girl and I wanted to be big like you today.'

The truth and sincerity in the little girl's statement turns things around. At first you connect with the mother and her struggle, and then somehow, suddenly, also with the little girl.

Emotions are made for communication. When they are simple and open, and expressed with a trust that they will be heard, they carry influence and weight. Some psychologists call emotions expressed in this way 'primary emotions', meaning that they are clear and open and unfiltered. Primary emotions might be described as heartfelt, in that they are straightforward and hopeful. They are fairly easy to recognize in that:

- They tend to pop up quickly and clearly and express themselves in simple terms. This is important because they help a child slow down his experiences and steady and orientate himself.
- They aren't defensive, rather they are open and trusting. They often being with an 'I'. '*I am sad*', '*I am frightened*', '*I worry that*'. The 'I' shows up because your child feels comfortable owning the emotions. He believes that these emotions will make sense to you and that you will be able to connect with him.
- They communicate their message effectively and clearly and then they pass. The simplicity and ease of these direct, open emotions means that they are good for using the right amount of energy for the job. They don't try and get something done through making others feel bad, or making something else the bad thing. They don't allow fear or

confusion to build up. Rather they open out experiences and shift and develop a child's understandings.

Sometimes we see such openness as naïve and weak. We associate this kind of expression with a younger child who hasn't yet learnt to be artful. Although such open, initial emotions are often expressed by younger children, they aren't weak. They are agile, responsive and expressive. Their directness and honesty means they clarify and open up situations. They slow things down and invite connection and support.

WHEN EMOTIONS BECOME CONFUSED, CONTROLLING AND STUCK

A child's ability to express his emotions with such directness and clarity is affected by many factors. In part, the process of maturing means that your child begins to learn more about social norms and the invisible rules around how we express ourselves. From about the age of eight or nine years there are pressures on a child to be more 'grown up' or less noisy and demanding. He comes to see such openness and vulnerability as childish.

He is also likely to learn at some point that emotions as inconvenient or awkward or annoying. These inconvenient emotions can communicate things that other people don't want to hear (*I'm tired, I'm lonely, I'm worried*) and so the emotions get pushed aside or quickly 'fixed', perhaps with a treat or distraction or an explanation as to why they can't be right. Your child will quickly pick up on this, learning how to distract, fix or divert emotions all by himself.

Fixing or managing emotions isn't necessarily a bad thing. After all, he spends a lot of time at school having to fit in, manage other children's behaviours, etc. and there are also the many times in normal family life when things are busy and jobs/homework/meals need to be organized. But it is important that a child has space during the day when his emotions are listened to and understood. This regular practice of making space for emotions, without fixing or distracting, means that when bigger, more painful emotions come along, your child knows you are able and ready to hear hard things and will try to understand and make space.

PUSHING AWAY EMOTIONS

Some years ago I met a mother and her daughter, Britta. She was nine and her parents had separated. Britta and her mum lived together with her baby brother. She saw her dad intermittently at the weekends. One weekend her dad had said he would pick her up at lunchtime on the Saturday and take her overnight to stay her grandmother's. Knowing that her dad often let her down, Britta's mother had played down the sleepover saying that they would go over to see some friends if her dad hadn't picked her up by 3pm.

At 3pm there was no sign of her dad. Britta's mum told Britta that they should go to the friend's house and that her dad could come and collect her from there. Britta seemed quiet and uncomplaining. She helped her mum with the baby's buggy and got her coat. As they made their way out of the house, Britta suddenly became furious. The baby had dribbled on her coat sleeve. Britta started shouting at the baby that he had ruined her coat, that it was disgusting. She pushed her mum away shouting that she wanted her and the baby to 'get lost'.

Britta's mum tried to reassure her that she had messaged her dad and let him know where to find them. That she would keep her phone near. Britta shouted through tears that she

didn't care about her dad, that this was not to do with him.
She stormed ahead down the road, ignoring her mother.

Talking to Britta's mother, I could see why Britta would want to push away the situation, but also why she wanted to push away the large emotions that sought to remind her and hook in her attention. Not seeing her dad or being able to rely on him was distressing. She certainly didn't want her emotions reminding her about him or this potential rejection.

A child who feels emotionally overwhelmed (disorientated, rejected, fearful) will instinctively take action to protect himself. When he can't protect himself from the situation, he does the next best thing: he tries to protect himself from the loud, painful emotions.

For Britta, filled with confused, loud emotional responses, she was left feeling there was no choice but to try and push them away. Unfortunately pushing away her emotions created an internal struggle that then left Britta feeling confused and defensive and powerless. Rather than settling her emotions, they got bigger and more confusing, pushing others away.

It's important to understand that even if the original event is difficult and distressing, the initial vulnerable emotion is safe and exists to allow a child to process and adjust to a situation. Unfortunately, when it gets pushed away, a child will begin to see this vulnerable emotion itself as uncomfortable or overwhelming. For example, he starts to feel anxious about anxiety, or fearful of sadness.

When a child pushes away the initial emotion, it doesn't go away. It stays around but shifts becoming more confused and more defensive. You'll see from the table below that being open and acknowledging the initial emotion allows it to express itself and pass. This is so much better than hiding it and giving rise to the defensive emotion.

INITIAL EMOTION	DEFENSIVE EMOTION
A simple reaction to an event (for example, vulnerability)	A reaction to the initial emotion (so for example, anger about feeling vulnerable)
Easy to understand (for example, sadness following the loss of a special toy)	Complicated or ambiguous (for example, rather than seeing the initial sadness, a parent will see anger or jealousy or meanness)
Open and communicative	Defensive and closed – your child pushes you away
Able to be expressed when a child feels connected to and understood by a parent	Comes about when a child feels overwhelmed and alone with a situation; when he feels it is linked to his own goodness and lovability
Brings others closer/allows empathy	Interferes with a child's ability to connect with you and your capacity to help him
Fades away over time	Continues even when the event has finished and gets stronger over time

Defensive emotions are confused and fearful. This fear makes them dominant and forceful. They are emotions in search of a quick, strong solution and they pull a child into a forceful struggle.

The tricky thing is that when emotions are confused and tight, they push others away. Your child begins to feel even *more* lost and ashamed and then more defensive. He gets stuck. He experiences his emotions as demanding, difficult and confusing. They make him feel bad. And so, he comes to believe that there must be something 'bad' about him. It's therefore important that you step in to help a child slowly soften and let go of these defensive emotions. You are the person who helps him slow down his defences, understand how they work and recognize the power of initial emotions in helping him connect with others and communicate his needs.

TALKING TO YOUR CHILD ABOUT BIG, DEFENSIVE EMOTIONS

To help a child understand what happens when he is experiencing big, defensive emotions, I often compare pushed away emotions to a beach ball pushed under the water. My aim is to help a child understand why pushed away emotions (even when they feel painful or confusing) can come back feeling so big. I normally say something along these lines:

'Have you ever had a beach ball in a swimming pool or in the sea and tried to push it under the water? The ball is big and light on the surface but when you try and push it down it takes a lot of effort. The funny thing is, the harder you push it down, the more forcefully it wants to push itself back up. And if you're not careful, it flies back up into your face in a crazily powerful way!

'Well, the beach ball is like your emotions. When you get upset and confused about an emotion, you might find yourself trying to push it away. For example, if you mess up playing football and your friends get annoyed at you, you feel wobbly and upset. You don't like feeling like this at school, so you try and push the emotion away. And the emotion acts like a beach ball. Firstly, it takes a lot of energy to push away – but then, instead of staying out of your head, it comes back with more energy. You might find yourself getting in a rage about another small thing or feeling overwhelmed and panicky throughout the match.'

A child will best relate to this metaphor in relation to the times when *you* or another adult have pushed away his feelings. These will be the times when you've provided quick solutions, not had time, felt cross or annoyed or disagreed with him that he feels a certain way. These incidences, rather than being problematic, can become important moments in his understandings. You might say, *'I'm sorry, I didn't listen to what you had to say. It must be really hard for you when your emotions don't get listened to.'* You can then tell him about the beach ball analogy and relate this back to how he felt.

The process of recognizing that he does this to his own emotions is a harder thing for a child to reflect upon since he is most likely to push his own emotions away instinctively; his need for the computer game/distraction is the only thing he is left being aware of.

The best way for him to learn how to give his emotions time is by experiencing you pausing to listen and understand his emotions (whether these are the initial emotion or the defensive emotion or the feeling that he needs to play a certain game). The beach ball analogy is best used as reflection and not in the context of trying to convince him he doesn't need specific distractions.

ACKNOWLEDGING AND WITNESSING EMOTIONS HELPS EMOTIONS TO SLOW AND SETTLE

Emotions often get pushed away for one reason or another. The important thing to bear in mind is that even defensive, tight emotions can slow down so that they become simpler and more open when a child has help to slow down and express himself. When you notice your child becoming upset or distressed:

- Witness the emotions (*'You're having a tough time, this feels difficult/upsetting/sad.'*)
- Allow them (*'You're trying so hard to explain how you feel, all of this makes sense.'*)
- Release (*'Let's sit down and give you some time. I'm here with you.'*)

Of course, this process is far easier when your child expresses the kind of open, vulnerable, slow emotions that we saw at the beginning of this chapter. However, if, as is often more likely, his emotions are fast, reactive and defensive emotions, you can still help. You might need to limit destructive or difficult behaviours, but you can listen carefully to what he says, acknowledging and allowing his feelings. When you don't try to block or push away his feelings, they become more balanced and reflective. They express themselves, they shift and they pass. Your child learns that he can be heard, that his experiences matter, that you are there for him.

POINTS TO REMEMBER

- **When your child feels comfortable expressing his emotions, he communicates simply and clearly**. He trusts that others will understand and support him. The emotion carries a clear message and passes.
- **Often, however, his emotions will get pushed away**. This can be because their message seems inconvenient or worrying. It can be because we get used to 'managing' and 'fixing' emotions.
- **'Pushed away' emotions, rather than disappearing, become tight and defensive and difficult to manage**. They hang around triggering difficult behaviour and further defensive reactions. Your child begins to feel ashamed of his emotions. He begins to struggle.
- **Your job is to help your child express and release the emotion**. This happens when you acknowledge or witness the emotion, allow or validate his experience and soothe and contain fear and disorientation.
- **When this happens, his defensive emotions slow down**. He begins to reflect on his feelings and is more able to settle and express his initial, more vulnerable emotions.

3

HELPING YOUR CHILD UNDERSTAND EMOTIONS

We ended chapter 2 by beginning to think about how you can help your child express and release defensive emotions. Although this process can sound simple, it can be surprisingly tricky and difficult. In this chapter I want to explain why helping a child stay with her more open vulnerable emotions is such a valuable skill, but also how you can notice and overcome the things that block this process.

WHEN EMOTIONS FEEL PAINFUL

One of the hardest things to do as a parent is to remain open when your child's emotions trigger tight, defensive emotions in you. This might be because your child is experiencing a difficult situation that is painful to watch (as was the case with Britta), it could be because you feel worn down or frustrated by her emotions, particularly in the context of a busy, demanding family life. Or maybe there is something about these emotions that reminds you of your own difficulties or unresolved issues. Your instinct is to push away the emotions quickly.

I'll start this chapter by taking you through how Britta's mother was able to help her daughter stay with her painful emotions and gradually develop her own, steadier understandings. We'll continue this chapter by considering more widely how you can help your child when her emotional reactions forcefully push you away or pull her attention toward disruptive behaviour. We'll think about helping her understand the many different emotions she feels and how to deal with conflicting emotions that can create shame and confusion.

So let's go back to Britta. Britta's mother was worried about the impact of her father's chronically unreliable behaviour. She wanted to make the situation somehow go away so that Britta didn't have to feel confused or upset, but despite her efforts Britta was struggling to manage.

When I met with her mother, we spoke about the importance of staying with Britta's emotions more, acknowledging and supporting her experiences. Whilst we were meeting she began to notice changes in her daughter. The first big change happened one Monday morning when she was walking with Britta to school. This is how her mother explained things:

'As we were walking to school, Britta said, "I feel like Daddy doesn't love me." I felt a strong, tight emotional tug and the urge to push this idea away. I had said many times to Britta, "No, he's just busy. He's probably got caught up in work. You know what he's like." But I could feel the courage and braveness that it must have taken Britta to bring this up. It didn't seem good enough or real enough to brush away her emotions. So I simply said, "That's how it feels to you when he doesn't come and we don't hear from him."

'And she nodded and tears ran down her cheeks, so we just stopped and went and sat down on a bench away from the road. And then she said, "Lena's mum and dad have split up and her dad sees her every weekend and he doesn't ever not come for her."

'And I said, "Oh Britta. I love you so much. And this is hard. Your dad's behaviour is confusing and unfair but you are a million kinds of brilliant."

'We sat there for a little while. Britta said, "I don't feel brilliant – I feel useless." I didn't say any more because I didn't want to keep pushing away Britta's feelings, but I think she felt heard because she put her head on my shoulder and wiped at her tears.

'Then the baby threw down his drink and Britta picked it up. She turned to me: "Come on, Mum, we have assembly today and they're bringing in a guide dog so I can't be late. And anyway, the baby will want his nap." So we walked to school and I gave her a hug again and she went in.'

Britta and her mother had lots of conversations after that. None of them were long and mostly Britta started them. She would say, 'Why doesn't Dad love me?' and her mother would remember to make sure she let Britta's pain or anxiety be heard without giving a quick answer. Her mother would listen and say something like, 'You're thinking about Dad and how he makes plans which he doesn't keep.'

Sometimes Britta would say, 'He is rubbish and disgusting and I never want to see him.' At other times, she cried and at other times, she said things like, 'I wish he could be like the other dads.'

This growing openness and ability to think about how she felt was an important process for Britta. Her emotions were working to orientate her. In this open state through exploring with her mother, Britta was able to steady and orientate herself. She didn't have to cover up the vulnerable, open emotions or move to defensive emotions to try to cope. There was nothing in Britta's mother's reaction that suggested that something was wrong with these reactions, or that Britta needed to change, or that more energy should be put into the situation. Britta was gradually developing an honest, truthful understanding that the situation was painful, but that she could be okay.

The upsetting emotions that Britta was feeling were there to help her try to make sense of the situation. In other words, they provide opportunities for growth and development.

THE EFFECTS OF FULLY ACKNOWLEDGING YOUR CHILD'S EMOTIONS

When a child's experiences and opinions are listened to and acknowledged, things change.

- She becomes more able to openly and directly express how she feels. She begins to be able to reflect on and understand her experiences with more openness and honesty.
- She has more ability to adjust and respond.
- She might feel sad or angry but not fearful or overwhelmed or ashamed.
- She can place more trust in those who can support and guide her.
- Her understandings of situations and relationships become more nuanced and subtle.
- She stops feeling so alone. Through sharing she might get to hear about other people's experiences and situations. She sees that she is not on her own.

In chapter 2 we looked at how emotions that are denied or pushed away can become defensive and stuck. In contrast, the more a child is listened to, the more she lets go of her frustrations and her fears and her confusion. She becomes more comfortable expressing her initial, open emotions. And importantly, although the situations she responds to can be difficult and upsetting, her emotions stay regulated and healthy.

YOUR ROLE IN HELPING YOUR CHILD OPEN UP HER EMOTIONS

Britta's mum noticed that she wanted to avoid her daughter's pain. She wanted to explain away and neutralize the dad's behaviour. To normalize it. To neatly take away those upsetting emotions. But she also recognized that there is a braveness in a child owning her vulnerable feelings.

The emotions a child experiences are there to help her clarify her thoughts and understand the situation fully. Passing over these emotions too quickly doesn't allow a child to properly open out her understandings and orientate. It gives the message that her emotions are wrong or need to be avoided or fixed.

Through giving time to emotions, a child gradually understands the things that she is responsible for but also the things that are beyond her control and not related to her goodness or worth. These things require big understandings which unfold slowly, once the initial emotions have been heard fully.

NOTICING YOUR DISCOMFORT AROUND EMOTIONS AND THE NEED TO FIX

So why do parents try and pass over a child's distress? There are many reasons and most of them are familiar and understandable:

- Open, vulnerable, direct emotions can leave parents feeling uncomfortable, guilty or pressurized and unsure how to respond.

- Parents want to make things right for a child straight away. They don't want their child to be hurt or harmed by things outside of her control. They fear she will be emotionally wounded or confused.
- These emotions can seem to be too negative. You worry that they will lead to difficult, frustrating behaviour.
- Sometimes parents are going through similar difficulties themselves. They can be affected by the same thing that their child is going through. They feel overwhelmed by their child's additional need and shocked or worried to see their emotions mirrored in their child.
- There can be a sense of weariness and tiredness around emotions. If a child has been struggling with defensive emotions, it can feel never ending and parents want these tricky emotions to go away.

Although discomfort occurs for many reasons, listening and supporting a child to think about her emotions gives you the opportunity to help her step away from further struggle and overwhelm. When you become aware of this inner struggle, you'll find you have the chance to adjust and shift your responses. Rather than instinctive avoidance and discomfort, you notice you can step back and allow yourself and your child more space and time to talk about the emotions. You might become aware of your own judgements about good or bad emotions – but instead of closing these emotions down, you focus on connecting with your child, helping her to feel safe and secure, listening to her experiences and opinions.

This process isn't easy but it's worth it. You might imagine that staying with – and acknowledging – your child's emotions will feel like you are letting her down, or not protecting her. The reality is that when you truly listen and understand, you notice how capable and steady her emotions can be. That you can help her gradually let go of fear and panic and find a much more truthful, balanced understanding, even when things around her are hard and uncertain.

'LEANING-IN' TO YOUR CHILD'S EMOTIONS

The thing about being emotionally open is that it can feel vulnerable and can take a great deal of courage for a child to try. If she has a sense that you will judge her negatively or be frustrated or anxious, she is likely to push away these brave emotions. It's therefore important that you stand back and pause judgement whilst listening and opening up to her emotions. We call this 'leaning-in' to the emotion.

This process is slow and can be challenging for all involved. By 'leaning-in', you allow your child to see her emotions for long enough to begin to understand and reflect on them. It will also allow the time for you to understand the emotions more, without jumping to conclusions about the cause or wider meaning.

Here are some examples of how we can replace the need to judge and move away from your child's emotions with slower, more open, connected responses:

Your child says: '*I felt sad when Analise wasn't in today.*'
Judgement response: '*Oh but there are so many other children you can play with.*'
'Leaning-in' response: '*You felt sad because she wasn't in....*'

Your child says: '*I hate Mummy when she gets really cross.*'
Judgement response: '*Well Mummy has had a lot to do today, and you need to help her out more.*'
'Leaning-in' response: '*You want me to know that you really don't like it when Mummy gets mad.*'

Your child says: *'I am scared of the dark.'*
Judgement response: *'There's nothing to be frightened of. You know I'm next door and you have your little light.'*
'Leaning-in' response: *'You feel frightened when it's dark…'*

Leaning-in to these emotions doesn't mean you're feeding into these feelings or intensifying them. Instead, you're communicating that you want to learn about her feelings, that you are comfortable, that they are meaningful.

When you lean-in, your child doesn't have to hold on to emotions. She can consider the feeling and then shift her position as she continues to think. She learns that her emotions have a message and that they can be opened up and slowly extended to bring further ease and clarity.

HOW TO COPE WITH EMOTIONS THAT SEEM TO PUSH YOU AWAY

Although you want to help your child with these initial, open emotions, they can be very fleeting. They pop up and then quickly get pushed away and covered up by defensive emotions (as in chapter 2). In fact, most of the emotions that you need to help your child with can end up being these defensive, confused emotions. These defensive emotions could be jealousy (your child might be very jealous of a new baby, not letting you cuddle him or play with him), frustration or anger (over small, seemingly inconsequential events such as getting her hair cut or going to buy new shoes), or worry around uncertainty (she might stubbornly refuse to go to bed because it's light outside and she will only go when it's dark).

These emotions are hard to connect to because:

- They can be difficult to understand or feel sympathy with.
- They aren't always linked to specific situations. In fact, they often happen habitually, for seemingly no particular reason.
- They can be attacking or mean or controlling.
- They repeatedly reappear without seeming to properly go away.
- They lead to tension and challenging, upsetting behaviours.

The temptation is to try to challenge or deny or forbid these defensive emotional reactions. Unfortunately, rather than go away, these emotions have a habit of getting larger and more frequent. The real solution comes through helping a child to slow down these emotions and open them out.

Instead of avoiding these emotions, you can:

- Recognize when you are being drawn into struggles or quick fixes with your child
- Learn how to connect to your child's defensive emotions
- Help your child to settle and regulate all of these tricky, awkward, confusing feelings.

To do this, you'll need to build your understanding of what is happening when your child experiences these defensive emotions. Only then, you can find a way through for you and your child. Let's look at how these emotions can play out and what you can do about it.

RESPONDING TO DISPLACED EMOTIONS

One of the most common reactions to confusing or overwhelming feelings is to displace them. Displacing emotions happens when a child shifts her focus onto something that feels safer and less threatening. We saw this with Britta, who was unable to express her anger or distress to her father and instead got cross with the baby. And with Ned in chapter 1, who responded to a situation he was embarrassed about by pushing his brother and blaming his toast.

Whilst displacing emotions in this way is extremely common, it can nonetheless be hard for a parent to manage. Displacing emotions can become very habitual so that the smallest twinge of a difficult emotion leads to a child redirecting her attention; perhaps to a sibling or parent but sometimes onto things such as objects, clothes, foods. Your child starts thinking of these 'innocent' things as frustrating or 'wrong'. Unhappily this displacement can also mean that, at the point when she needs more connection, your child ends up being told off or disciplined because her behaviour seems unreasonable and unnecessarily difficult.

So, what can be done about these displaced emotions? You might feel frustrated at your child's insistence that she 'hates' all of her toys or thinks her younger brother is 'horrible and mean'. You try and ignore it or maybe gently point out the thing that might have *really* made her upset to begin with. Most of the time however you get caught in trying to manage and limit these confusing and difficult responses. You want your child to see her behaviour as wrong or nonsensical. You get pulled into battle.

Whilst it's important to limit behaviours which are damaging or hurtful, it's also essential to find a way to connect to these displaced emotions. Children can displace an emotion onto a person or onto a need for something. Your job is to gently stand in and help them reconnect back to you, so that they can work through the emotion rather than getting lost in the short-term distraction they are looking for. Let me give you an example:

Your child is upset because her friend was nasty to her at school. She gets home and becomes very angry when you say she can't go on the computer. She throws the iPad down.

First, establish a secure, safe boundary around destructive behaviours:

You: 'I don't want the iPad to get damaged, I'm going to take it to keep it safe.'
Then lean-in to what's really going on:
You: 'Tell me what's bothering you.'
Child: 'I want to play on the iPad and you won't let me of course!'
You: '... And you feel really annoyed.'
Child: 'Yes, you're stupid and I hate you.'
You: 'You're having a bad time today...'
Child: (shrugs but half nods)
You: (Move in near to her and listen)

Often it isn't necessary to ask another question; rather you can put a hand on her shoulder or gently brush a little bit of hair away from her face. The most important thing is to stop her emotions from being displaced onto quick fixes or difficult behaviours and to give her time to stay with the emotion and open it out.

She may or may not say more but she feels the connection to you and your kindness and openness. This opens the way for something to perhaps come out later, when she feels less tight and defensive. Although this approach takes a bit of time, it actually saves times because it stops a situation escalating, it gets to the root of the problem and prevents the need for further discipline.

UNDERSTANDING THE MEANING OF 'I HATE YOU'

Notice in the example above that I don't suggest reacting to words such as 'I hate you'. A child will often say something akin to '*I hate*'. Their meaning is very different to the adult meaning, which is strong and severe.

'Hate' tends to be said when a child feels frustration or a loss of control. Underlying this statement is her confusion around a situation. She doesn't know what to do and she doesn't have the emotional literacy to communicate in a more open, mature way.

If you were to react to these sorts of statements with punishments or reprimands, your child experiences the excitement of a word which seems powerful and important. Everyone's attention would divert away from the original emotion and things would become more complicated and confusing.

The best thing, if a child isn't hurting someone or causing damage, is to see the vulnerability behind this type of statement and let her express herself.

ACCEPT THAT EMOTIONS CONSTANTLY SHIFT

Although a child will talk about things and her emotions seem to settle, it is completely usual for these emotions to become unsettled again and again. Perhaps she has additional pressures on her (for example school pressures or a growth spurt), maybe her understandings are growing and adapting to new information. Whilst it can seem like Ground Hog Day, each time your child is able to relate, to slow down and be with these emotions, she is getting steadier and her emotional intelligence is growing. She becomes more able to deal with difficulties and distressing emotions.

DON'T OVER-ANALYSE OR TRY AND INSIST ON VULNERABILITY

To recap, you step in to limit the amount your child can displace an emotion (e.g. you prevent her yelling at siblings or grabbing the computer) and you show through your warm, steady presence that you are there for her. But – and this is important – you don't insist or force her to tell you what the matter *really* is.

When you're anxious about a child's emotions it is sometimes tempting to check in on your child's emotions, prompting her, or suggesting feelings and responses. Although this is well intentioned, it can backfire. Let me give you an example:

You're having a difficult time with your daughter. You told her that you would have to go away for a couple of days at short notice and she had become silly, messing around in the bathroom and then began shouting at you when you tried to step in.

You're sure it's to do with you going away as this has been difficult for her before.

You: 'Are you feeling worried because I'm going away?'
Child: 'No. You can do whatever you like. I don't care.'
You: 'I think you might be annoyed or cross at me because you had a bad time before.'
Child: 'I'm not annoyed. I told you, you can do what you like.'
You: 'It's going to be okay you know, it's only until Friday and...'
Child: 'Can you stop saying that. I DON'T CARE!'

Rather than helping a child or reassuring her that she can talk things through, that you are able to hear and learn about her feelings, these conversations can trigger her upset. She feels unsettled and unprepared. She instinctively hides the emotion; and pulls away more.

A child's readiness to reflect on her emotions has its own particular time frame. You can prompt her by reflecting yourself:

You: 'This going away suddenly hasn't given me much time to make a plan with you about how we check in each day. Let's have a think about that.'

You might share similar experiences to hers, perhaps from your childhood, but be careful to leave a space between your story and her experience. Trust that if you are calm, steady, open and supportive when she initiates conversations that she will talk to you if she needs to. Slowly she'll become more comfortable bringing things to you. And if she doesn't, well you simply keep listening and sharing and connecting to her experiences.

A NOTE ON ANXIOUS OR PANIC-BASED EMOTIONS

Some emotions, such as those which are panic-based, are difficult for a child to 'think' her way through, even with your open support and connection. These emotions throw her thoughts around, constantly refocusing her on uncertainty and fear.

When your child is feeling high levels of panic or anxiety, rather than focusing on talking, it's helpful to support her in stepping away from her thoughts. Instead, shift her attention into her physical body, or if that's too hard, onto you and the environment around her.

You can say: *'These thoughts and feelings are so hard. They're bouncing around, but you're safe here with me.'*

Helping her make sense of this experience can happen at a later point when she feels steadier, when her thoughts are less likely to race ahead.

SEEING ALL THE EMOTIONAL PARTS

The more a child experiences her emotions being acknowledged and treated as valid, the more she understands the different emotions she experiences, the way they shift and move and communicate different needs and perspectives. She notices that she can have many feelings, sometimes contradictory, sometimes all at the same time. For example, she loves her brother – she enjoys spending time on the trampoline with him, but she also finds him boring sometimes... and repetitive... and silly. She wishes she had a sister but is also glad to be the only girl in the family.

These more nuanced emotions help her understand and appreciate the world. They deepen her experience and help her make sense of situations that are complex and multifaceted.

Let's take the experience of sadness for example. When your child feels sad because her friend moves to another school, she gains a greater sense of the importance of relationships. She appreciates the connections she had with that friend but also her links to others more generally. Other so-called negative emotions also help her value and appreciate things. For example, her experience of loss motivates her to remember and celebrate. Loneliness perhaps prompts her to open up and communicate. Guilt makes her take more care.

Although she can become relatively sophisticated in her understandings, some situations place demands that are beyond her emotional capabilities particularly at around the age of nine or ten years, as she starts to become more independent and spends a greater amount of time at school or with friends. Whereas before she relied on your close help, the pressures of growing up and becoming more independent mean that she is dealing with ever more complex situations and trying to pull together emotional responses that she only partially understands and can't fully articulate.

These emotional responses might be the different 'adult' emotional reactions she has experienced, but doesn't yet completely understand, full of 'should' and 'should-nots'. They may be impulsive emotions – to run away or shout or lie. Or emotions she has seen friends trying out, such as jealousy, loyalty, being offended, being embarrassed. Managing these different emotional responses, with all the different directions they push her in can begin to feel bewildering and difficult, particularly when she is under pressure. Without guidance, a child is likely to get confused, unable to move beyond simply performing these emotions.

When I am explaining how these different emotional responses interact and get confused, I often tell a story from my own childhood where my own young, immature emotional responses were put under pressure:

In this story I am about nine years old and I am walking home from school. An older man is sitting on a wall. As I walk past, he calls out to me that I have something on my shoe. I can't see anything, but he is insistent that there is a mark and he comes to show me, putting my foot with the 'dirty' shoe on his lap so that he can clean it.

I feel very uncomfortable and confused. On the one hand I know that I shouldn't talk to strangers or accept lifts; that I should quickly walk away if a someone asks me if I want to see some puppies. But on the other hand, I also know I should be respectful and polite to adults that offer help.

So I stay put. The man rubs my shoe vigorously and all the while my brain is shouting both that I don't like this, that I want him to stop, but also that this isn't a good enough reason and that he is helping. I am stuck. Luckily, a family friend walks toward us. 'What are you doing, Anne?' she asks sharply. The man lets go of my foot.

When I get home, I look at my shoe, scanning it for marks. There aren't any. I think, 'Mum would be so cross with me if she found out I'd spoken to a stranger and let him rub my shoe.' I feel silly and vulnerable and confused. I keep the incident to myself.

HELPING YOUR CHILD RECOGNIZE AND BALANCE DIFFERENT EMOTIONS

On that afternoon there were many different emotions trying to influence my behaviour:

- There were my 'wanting to be peaceful' emotions. The emotions that were respectful to adults, who believed that this man would surely know better. These emotions were more familiar as I often used them at school.
- Then there were the fearful emotions that felt unsafe and uncomfortable. They were loud but were unsure what I should do. They wanted more information and a way of getting away that wouldn't feel dangerous.
- At the same time, there were the painful, wounded emotions, including shame and confusion. They took up a lot of energy and pulled me into myself.
- Lastly, there were the protective/defensive emotions that wanted to cover up, to feel in control and to push all of this away.

Deciding which emotion should most influence my response felt impossible. Should it be the need to please adults? Or perhaps my own preference not to have my foot held and rubbed. Maybe I should be concerned not to annoy a man who was obviously stronger and more in control? This adult's behaviour was inappropriate and frightening. It must have been very scary for me at that age. Without access to an adult's experience and judgement, I didn't know how to manage the situation. I felt paralysed and overwhelmed.

One of the most difficult things about this situation is that I felt ashamed of my reactions. The shame stopped me telling my parents what had happened and meant that they couldn't help to keep me safe in the future. A child needs to be able to speak about her experiences without being held back by shame and confusion.

Showing your child that emotions can be made sense of; that they can be listened to, that their perspective and message is important even when they confuse and worry her, gives her this bridge to you and your care and protection.

In my situation I wasn't with my parents and I didn't tell them what happened. Earlier in this chapter we looked at how our discomfort as parents and our need to take action can come across as judgement and can silence a child. Your growing child will spend increased amounts of time without you by her side. It's therefore crucial that you make sure she comes to understand you as someone with whom she can share her concerns and difficulties and confusions, and is able to absorb a sense of openness, comfort and security around all emotions.

Here are some ways to help ensure this happens:

MAKING SENSE OF ALL EMOTIONS

Some emotions are easy to make sense of. If a child is bullied, it's simple enough to understand that she might feel worried and fearful of the bully and therefore reluctant to go into school or out into the playground. But sometimes her behaviour makes less sense, it can seem to conflict with what you would expect.

This behaviour will be underpinned by emotions that are more hidden. Your job is to try and help your child express the emotions underlying this behaviour without dismissing or judging them, so that she can communicate her needs and adapt her responses.

An example of this could be your child's behaviour when she has been teased and excluded by another child. Your child's responses are muddled. Sometimes she ignores the child, seeking to stay away and avoid her, but often she seems to seek that child out despite saying that she wants him to leave her alone. If you were to ask her why she does this, she might come up with an ad hoc explanation that doesn't make much sense.

To support her to open out and make sense of these different emotional responses, you might ask: *'Sometimes you stay out of Arthur's way but other times you move nearer to him. Can you remember what the different thoughts are in your head as you try to decide what to do each day?'*

If your child only repeats the reasons for staying out of Arthur's way, then be mindful that the emotions bringing her back closer to him might be more instinctive and harder for her to articulate.

You might gently say something like: *'Often we move closer or further away from someone because our feelings are trying to decide what to do. We can't always understand or put this into words very easily at first, but with practice we get better at understanding and working things out.'*

WORKING THROUGH SHAME

It's important when you are talking to your child to recognize that all her emotional responses have good intentions. They are trying to sort through situations and to help and protect her – even the defensive, tight, angry responses.

If you criticize a child's emotional responses, they get pushed to the side but they don't go away. Instead, she tries to sort out how to respond to that emotion without acknowledging or paying attention to it. The emotion doesn't get to express itself properly. It gets stuck and her behaviours become tight and confused as she tries to manage.

Once a child begins to feel ashamed of an emotional reaction, she tightens up when you talk about it. If you feel your child is pulling away, then the best thing to do is to step back and soften the focus.

You might say, *'It can be so tricky to work out emotions. They sometimes surprise us or take us in a direction which we later feel confused about.'*

Sometimes I tell children about the funny, surprising, baffling ways in which my emotions respond. How I intend to do one thing and find myself doing another. I take care to point out how these emotions are aiming to help me, and how I can help them to relax and work in a more supportive way by listening to them and thanking them for their help.

When emotions are responded to with open comfort, although your child might push away discussions around one area, she nonetheless becomes more open about other confusions and complications.

CONDUCTING AN ORCHESTRA OF EMOTIONS

Although your child is growing in abilities and independence, it is essential that she can take her experiences to you and use you to support and reflect.

I have heard psychologists with a background in Internal Family Systems Therapy (IFS) use the analogy of a conductor when referring to how parents help a child with all of the different emotional responses she experiences.

So if we think of parents as helping a child to conduct an orchestra of different emotions: To lead an orchestra, the conductor needs to bring out the different instruments and their different sounds. Sometimes the sound is more harmonious; at other times it's more dynamic and creative. With a conductor, the music has direction, it communicates openly and coherently. It makes sense.

As you assist your child, you help her notice and listen to her different emotional parts, bringing them out and allowing each to take up space and shift things, before balancing it again with the whole. With all her emotional parts having a role, she develops a fuller picture of the world. Her well-expressed emotions give her a deeper sense of the things that are important to her. She can begin choosing how to respond based on her values and preferences, rather than relying on instinctive, defensive responses.

POINTS TO REMEMBER

- **Listening and making space for your child's emotions can be difficult:**
  - Sometimes his emotions are painful and difficult to hear.
  - Sometimes his emotions push you away.
  - Sometimes his emotions are confusing – they can become displaced onto other things. This means that he pushes the emotion onto something external, for example he feels confused or upset but becomes cross with the dog.
- **When you begin to notice the things that push you away from his emotions you can adjust and shift your responses**. You recognize the importance of acknowledging and connecting to all of his emotions, even the defensive, frustrated ones.
- You learn to **limit his difficult or disruptive behaviour** whilst keeping the emotional connection to him **open and strong**.
- **Together, you begin to understand how nuanced and varied his emotions are**. He becomes more able to sort through his emotions and responds more confidently.
- **When you take a stance of 'Your emotions are important', 'I want to know about them', 'We can make sense of how you feel'**, he comes to trust that he can open up to you emotionally. He lets go of shame and reconnects to you. As he grows older, he knows he can share confusions, worries and difficult experiences with you and you will help him to make sense of his reactions and the emotions he feels.

4

GOOD ENOUGH PARENTING

*"Oh my darling it's true. Beautiful things have dents
and scratches too."*
Unknown

If your household is anything like my household, your ability to listen and acknowledge your child's emotions will have been put to the test numerous times already today. And if you are like me, you will have failed this test numerous times. Life with children is never smooth, easy or obvious. Just as your child can feel defensive and tight, so too can you. Just as she feels panicked and rushed, so too can you.

Luckily, your child's emotional development was designed to happen in the real world. Not in a world of serene, calm, capable adults, but in a world of busy, preoccupied, tetchy, worried, real adults who try hard but who often get it wrong.

The concept of the Good Enough Parent is essential to a child's developing EQ because it is real, because it is honest and because it will allow your child's emotions to learn and adjust, to become agile and resilient.

So, before we go on to Part Two and begin exploring each of the five steps, let's consider what Good Enough Parenting looks like and why it will provide such an important foundation to your parenting around emotions.

PERFECT PARENTING?

*My friend was sitting on the toilet, typing out a text.
'Mummy.' Her daughter's face peered through the crack in
the door. 'I can't see you. What are you doing?'*

*'Meieee,' mimics her little son, also standing outside.
'Eye cayne see oooh'.*

With determination they prize open the door.

*'Mummy's busy,' says my friend, trying unsuccessfully to
push back the door with her foot.*

'But Mummy, I'm bored,' says her daughter.

*The little one squeezes his way past his sister and
moves over to the side of the toilet. He peers down the
gap between my friend's bottom and the toilet seat.*

*'What's on your phone?' asks her daughter, peering at
the screen. She pokes at the send button on the message.*

*'Oh no!' says my friend crossly. 'Right, you two, I need
some peace. Out! Now!'*

Her son's face crumples.

'Mummy, you're horrid,' says her daughter crossly.

*Later that evening my friend recounted the episode to a
neighbour who had popped around.*

*'I can't wait for Dave to get back. I'm so exhausted. Not
only do my children constantly interrupt my thoughts,' she
complained 'but they also crowd out my physical space. I
can't even poo without company.'*

*'Hmm,' said the neighbour, thinking. 'Maybe they need
to feel they can rely on you. I mean they're obviously
feeling a bit insecure with their dad away. Perhaps they
just want that physical sense of your presence.'*

*'So now I'm exhausted and overwhelmed and guilty,'
moaned my friend to her husband when he arrived
home later.*

'Perhaps it's that the children find you quite entertaining – particularly when it involves poo!' he laughed.

When you're a new parent your sense of connection to your baby can be intense. I remember a health visitor explaining to a group of new parents how they could make the bed without putting the baby down. I often hear stories of new parents sitting at the bottom of their child's cot for hours whilst the baby slept, in case she woke up and felt momentarily alone and abandoned. Parents of new babies wonder how they will ever find the time to make themselves a cup of tea, let alone read or have a full conversation without the baby taking centre stage.

And then, slowly, as the demands of the world push their way back into consciousness, parents begin The Juggle. The postman keeps them waiting at the door waiting for a parcel whilst the baby cries. The dinner needs to be cooked, showers taken. The baby seems fine, or not so fine, but it's just short periods of time. They rush back and forth. Gradually their own temperament, capacity and parenting style become more established. There are the times when they feel grumpy or slow and there are the other days where they can be more responsive or lively.

Although the parent–child relationship starts with an intense feeling of connectedness, this state shifts and parents begin to move in and out of connection. When a parent is properly tuned into their child's emotional needs, they are referred to as being 'in sync'.

Being in sync means a parent is tuned in and responsive to a child's needs. For example, the periods when a child wants interaction and a parent stops and smiles and chats with her; the times when the child is hungry and her parents respond quickly to feed her; or the occasions when she wants to be held and soothed and a parent picks her up to comfort and reassure her.

Before you panic about how often you feel you are in sync with your child, know this: psychologist Ed Tronick and his team (Tronick et al, 1986) estimate that healthy adult–infant relationships are only in sync between 20 and 30 percent of the time. The rest of the time is spent 'in movement'. Moving out of sync, being out of sync, moving back into being in sync.

The periods where parents and children were out of sync are described as 'disconnections' or 'gaps'. Rather than thinking of these disconnections as simply negative, Tronick's team became aware of the many different meanings of these disconnections. Some of the gaps were difficult and unsettling; others were gentler and lower key. The team observed:

- Confused times, when a child tries to communicate an emotional need and the parent's response and awareness is mismatched. For example, the child wants to be reassured but her parent is trying to distract her or move away.
- Emotionally difficult times, when a parent felt rushed, frustrated or actively cross and the child felt uncertain, nervous or upset.
- Times when a parent moved temporarily out of sync to place boundaries around a behaviour either through a 'no' or through more actively stepping in.
- But also the times when a parent and child were attending to different things. For example, rather than being by her side helping, her parent was involved with another activity whilst the child played or explored.

It can be easy to assume that the more 'in sync' and connected a relationship is, the better. After all, we have already explored how connection repairs upset, helps a child understand emotions and feels safe and good. But interestingly (and thankfully), rather than the gaps creating a downwards spiral of disconnection and withdrawal, the reality is that these real relationships, full of gaps, miscommunications and complicated, wonky, loving exchanges, provide lots of surprising opportunities for emotional learning, newness, reconnection and repair. Rather than being a *problem*, when the relationship is secure enough, this shifting state of connection and disconnection allows your child to develop more agile, tuned-in emotional states.

Parents often find this research very healing and helpful. Inevitably you will have times where you are limited, snappy, busy or simply distracted and so it can be tremendously helpful to understand how you can help both yourselves and your child develop through these shifts and changes, gaps and difficulties. This can go a long way in alleviating any guilt you feel around this.

Let's look at how these shifting gaps and mismatches work their way through and serve the emotional needs of both you and your child.

BALANCING SPACE AND CONNECTION

The moving in and out of intimacy and connection that Tronick and his team saw is a natural, normal part of your relationship with your child. It has the potential to balance two very important emotional needs:

- Your child's need for security and safety, for reconnection and understanding and comfort
- Her equal need for a gradually opening space in which she can try out her own skills, gain confidence, settle to her own interests and work out her own preferences and capacities

Learning to ease into the relationship, to be in synchrony, happens best when things shift and adapt: when the gaps in the relationships aren't seen as mistakes, but rather adjustments and necessary spaces, and when the reconnections are enjoyed and frequent.

At its best, your relationship to your child helps to shape this space. She learns to move in and out of connection with you, what it means to be with you and without you and how she can bring you closer and make you understand her needs. Rather than a perfect, in sync relationship, the connection is constantly shifting with you both slowly finding your own ease and pace.

GOOD ENOUGH

Paediatrician and psychoanalyst Donald Winnicott described healthy relationships, with their manageable gaps and reconnections, as providing a 'good enough' experience for the child. 'Good enough' means that there is plentiful connection and repair and, importantly, that gaps are at a level that the child can cope with. In other words, the gaps are relatively small and familiar and the repairs or reconnections with a parent are easy and reassuring.

A typical example of the kind of thing that might have happened with your child when she was younger would have been that you were busy and her lunch was delayed. Perhaps she would have been upset and you would have talked to her about the situation ('*You're feeling hungry and there's been a little wait*') and after a bit of a juggle, you would have sat in front of her with her beans on toast. '*Oh sweetie*', you say, wiping her eyes and kissing her head. '*Here it is. There's no worry. It's here.*' Through this little gap and the not-too-delayed repair, your child would have learnt that she was able to cope, that the gap was okay, that you are trustworthy (if slow). The food had finally arrived and she had felt better.

As she got older, her resilience and independence increased and these gaps got gradually longer. She was able to get herself some fruit. She could ask you how long dinner was going to be. Slowly (as I explain later) she also learnt about the times when there is a break in the relationship; when you snapped or became frustrated or when she had a need that wasn't easily dealt with or worked through.

As we shall see, these real-world situations, rather than creating an ever-increasing gap or problem, were met with repairs and reconnections that strengthened, rather than weakened her emotional confidence and security.

LEARNING THROUGH THE GAPS

We often have a rather simplistic understanding of development, but there is a paradox at the heart of growth and learning. To learn about anything, we have to first know what it *isn't*. So, for a child to understand connection, she also needs to have an experience of space and separation.

Luckily, the continuous shifts found in good-enough relationships draw in her attention to the gaps and provide this useful contrast. In her growing relationship with you, your child experiences something different in the gaps. She experiences the loss of you and then the pleasure of reunion. Through these gaps she comes to know the value and need for connection. As she feels the vulnerability of aloneness, she comes to understand the security of connection.

In these gaps she is learning what she needs. She sees that you are separate but that she can move closer to you and that the gap can be overcome. Sometimes, the gap begins to feel stressful, and so in contrast the reconnection feels like release. With your presence, her system calms and regulates. Your presence comes to signal safety and change.

It is in this way that the shifts and changes, gaps and reunions in imperfect relationships help to sensitize, shape and orientate your child. Her emotions notice when the gap has become too big, she feels uncomfortable and looks for you. When she has your connected attention back, her system calms and regulates. Similarly at those times that she needs space, her emotions seek gaps and opportunities for space. She moves away, wanting to direct her own attention and focus.

Over time, your child learns to notice and respond to both types of need. Rather than being worried or preoccupied by gaps, she becomes more emotionally skilful and comfortable initiating connections and repairing these gaps herself.

POINTS TO REMEMBER

- **Psychologists often think about 'Good Enough Parenting' as the best type of parenting for a child's healthy emotional development**.
- **Good Enough Parenting is not about always being emotionally available, or never seeing to your own needs**. It describes *real* parent–child relationships.
- **In this real relationship there will be times when you and your child are emotionally connected and close, but also times when there are gaps**. Gaps can be because you or your child are immersed or busy with other things or they can happen when mistakes are made, emotions are heightened, and feelings are hurt.
- **When parenting is Good Enough, misunderstandings and hurt emotions are recognized, acknowledged and repaired readily**. When gaps get too big, you notice and reconnect back to your child.
- **Rather than failing a child, these gaps and mistakes and less-than-perfect interactions provide many opportunities**. She learns about the emotional reconnections and repairs that happen in healthy relationships. This increases her ability to adapt. She gains understanding and resilience.

5

EMOTIONAL REPAIRS

The relationship through which your child learns about emotions is constantly shifting. Rather than negatively affecting her EQ, these gaps give her the opportunity to start to understand others, their responses, their needs and her role in relationships. She becomes more emotionally agile and adept.

To help your child adapt to a world of imperfect, wobbly relationships and reconnections, it's useful to understand how a child learns to connect to us and how we can strengthen these reconnections to help her understand limits, grow more confident in her abilities, acknowledge hurt and emotional distress and repair gaps.

BIDS FOR CONNECTION

One of the things that happens when a child becomes confident and rewarded by relationships, is that she becomes interested in helping shape and develop these connections with those around her. Her efforts to do this are often described as 'emotional bids'.

I remember when my brother was about two years old. He was little, little enough that only his head peaked over the top of the table. Mum was sitting next to him. She was talking, but not to him.

'Mumma?' He looked up at her, squirming from side to side. His eyes darted around the table. He looked up at her again.

'Mumma?'

My mum is a lively conversationalist, and she was in full flow. Her conversation was aimed at a friend who was standing by the kettle, ready with a waiting teapot.

'Mumma?' My brother twisted his whole body around. He stretched his neck and tilted his face up toward her.

The kettle bellowed smoke. Mum's eyes were on the teapot. She was still talking.

'Mumma?' Determined to her get her attention he turned himself around to kneel on the chair. Reaching up he tilted Mum's face around so that she could see him.

'Mumma?'

My mum smiled down at him.

My brother had to work hard for this connection. And in our busy family the responses weren't always positive or smooth. My mum might easily have told him to wait or noticed a smudge on his face so that the attention would have turned to wiping and cleaning. But my brother had a general enjoyment and pleasure in his relationships that would have made this bid worth his effort.

A young child's bids will be basic. She might attempt to connect through her gaze (trying to catch your eye), by putting her arms out or by calling or crying.

Sometimes as a child gets older, the emotional openness and vulnerability shown by a younger child gets pushed out of the way. It exists as a small chat and cuddle at bedtime but otherwise for the rest of the day she remains mostly independent and distracted. There are many reasons for this. It can be because she learns that it seems babyish to ask for a cuddle. Or it can be because, in the rush of everyday life, the 'norm' is for her physical needs to be prioritized and there are no clear pathways for emotional need. This gets echoed in her playtimes when her interactions are predominantly through screens and computers.

When a child *does* notice her need for emotional connection, her bids for this connection have lost their ease and immediacy. Her bids might become tight and abrupt. Rather than being able to use relationships to adapt and develop emotionally, she may become stuck and isolated. It's therefore important that you provide the space and encouragement to support these bids when they do happen.

WHEN CHILDREN STRUGGLE TO CONNECT

At one of the residential units I worked in, I got to know an eight-year-old boy called Luca. He had a great mop of jet-black hair and a funny habit of putting on all of the tops he could find in his drawer, one over the other, so that he ended up looking like he'd been stuffed into them. Luca's way of trying to emotionally connect with me when we met was quite jarring. He would run to head butt my back. When I would look around to say hello, he would stick out his tongue. Quite often he would shoot me with a pretend gun shouting, 'You're sooo dead!' and run away.

Luca's abrupt attempts at engagement made it hard for adults to relate and respond effectively to him. He was often told off or corrected for being too rough or annoying. Rather than helping him develop softer or easier ways of connecting with others, his behaviour seemed to become more jarring and difficult to respond to. He was stuck anxiously wanting connection, but also wanting to cover up his vulnerability with fast, silly behaviours.

Relationships are the most important way for a child to regulate difficult or disorientated emotions. When a child feels an easy connection to an adult, her emotions settle and slow. Luca's difficulty connecting to others meant that his emotions were choppy and hard for him to regulate. It was important that he gained confidence in his bids to connect to me.

In order to help him, the first thing I did was to give Luca time to come slowly in, rather than dismiss his behaviours as silly or problematic. If I gave him my full attention, gently mimicking him by sticking out my tongue just a bit, then giving a ready smile, he seemed to relax a bit and orientate back to me. It required me to stop, to give him time, to show very clearly that I was pleased to see him and that I could relate to him. This was a challenge in a very busy, demanding unit. But it meant he approached me more often, and most importantly, he had a felt sense of the interaction, of being prioritized, being liked, being related to.

As Luca settled more, we would talk about how people responded to him and what he thought about these responses – whether he found the interactions awkward, fun, interesting or difficult. Tellingly, he noticed a lot about how others reacted (although he tended to report this in an offhand kind of way to let me know he wasn't so bothered). For example, he told me: 'Jay looked at me funny' or 'You (Anne) touched my head and that messed my hair', or 'Val kept asking me questions.'

Gradually, he began to talk about his own feelings, behaviours and attempts at interaction alongside his observations of others. He made comments such as: 'He was angry. I could tell because he wouldn't look at me but he had to laugh because my dance was so funny'; 'I helped her carry the tray up the stairs and she said, "Thank you very much, Mr Luca," in a singing voice.' 'I remembered stories about my weekend because you (Anne) like me to tell you about those, but sometimes they are not good.'

In this way, Luca began noticing the funny, quirky, changeable nature of relationships and the emotions that these revealed. I could see his confidence grow. His understanding and reflection gave him a way of navigating and shifting his own responses. No longer would he try to find his way through awkward and clumsy bids; rather his bids were becoming more agile and he was beginning to enjoy himself. His emotional range and ability to respond easily and fluidly was growing.

Many children can have difficulties similar to Luca's. Sometimes as they get older, they want more independence and feel more awkward connecting; at other times, they have a background of difficult relationships, they carry a sense of defensiveness and protection into their interactions.

HOW TO ENCOURAGE OPEN BIDS FOR CONNECTION

Given that your child will use her relationship with you to adapt and develop emotionally, it's important to know how to help her become more comfortable and open in her bids.

Let's look at ways in which you can facilitate this.

Recognize That Most Interactions are 'Bids'

Sometimes they are jarring and clumsy, but once you recognize these efforts to connect, you can make space for them and help them to become slower and easier. Bids might look like: shooting you with a pretend gun; telling you in detail about Star Zombies and Space Wars; telling you she's bored; grabbing you; making random noises at you; saying something hurtful or complaining.

Stop and Connect

When you accept your child's bids for connection and respond to them with ease, they soften and adapt. Your child is able to become more easy and confident in connecting. The best way to respond and help her shape a bid is for you to stop what you're doing, slow down and move nearer.

Mirror or Copy Behaviour

Mirroring or copying physically clumsy or jarring bids, in a gentler, slower way, with a small smile helps her to see these attempts in a more relaxed context. She also feels noticed, held by your attention and connected with.

Help 'Shape' the Bid

Some bids can be 'shaped' to lead to actual connection.

Your child might start telling you a long and boring story in mesmerizing detail. You can reflect back to her, '*The funny parts make you laugh*', '*You want me to know just how funny this is so we can laugh together*', '*There seem so many little details popping into your mind, it must be difficult trying to remember and explain at the same time*'. Reflecting back in this way helps her see what she might really want to convey and share. It brings her back to the relationship and her connection with you rather than her efforts turning into another form of disconnection.

If your child's bids seem to involve a lot of requests (for help, snacks or because she is 'bored'), prioritize talking and connecting with her over the help. So, if she wants a plaster for a small cut then rub her back, stroke her hair, chat to her in general and take your time with the plaster. The plaster is the excuse to get your attention for the real connection desired. It's a quick fix for you at a busy time, but does not address the root of the issue.. We shall look at this in more detail below.

WHEN BIDS TURN INTO FIXES

In chapter 4, we established that relationships are imperfect – and this is not actually a bad thing. They are complicated and messy and there are gaps and disconnections between parents and children. Bids for reconnection work to reinstate the emotional link between you and your child.

Although bids can become distorted by uneasiness or a lack of confidence in the relationship (as we saw with Luca), they can also become weakened when the bid for connection gets turned into a bid to fix something. Rather than repairing a gap or difficulty, the fix takes attention away from the relationship.

All parents are guilty of this; it comes with the busyness of life. An example of the way in which a fix can take over from a relationship repair happened with me and my son.

I promised my three children ice lollies after school. Having found three lollies that I was sure they all liked I discovered that my son was unhappy. He had wanted a different lolly and he felt very aggrieved.

That night as I was working, he came to find me. 'Mummy,' he said, 'I felt so sad about the lolly and you got cross and didn't go and get another one.'

I'm quite receptive to these kind of late evening visits (within reason). They feel like opportunities to repair a sadness or relationship break with connection and comfort. But on this particular evening, my son seemed to be replacing the connection with a push for a more practical solution to the upsetting lolly incident. He told me in detail how I could have got him a Double Choco Mega Ice Bar. I listened carefully, acknowledging all the details.

'So tomorrow can we go straight after school and get one?' he finished as he sat on my lap fiddling with my computer mouse.

'Hmmm,' I said, absorbing this not very appealing fix.

'And then I won't feel bad,' he concluded comfortably.

'Do you know how much I like you sitting here with me?' I asked.

He shrugged.

'I love you. And I was so happy at the idea of you and your brother and sister having some tasty ice lollies. And then it went a bit wrong and I felt a bit sad. As the evening moved on and we kept arguing about it I felt grumpy.'

'So can we get a Choco Mega tomorrow?' he asked quickly.

'I think... we should leave it this week,' I said looking at him sadly.

'Oh Mummy!' he said sorrowfully.

'It does feel a bit miserable,' I said.

He put his head on my chest and I put my arm around him.

'Perhaps next week when I'm doing the online order we can look at some of the lollies that are available and order some that everyone would like,' I suggested.

He nodded. 'Mummy, sometimes you are annoying and sometimes you have okayish good ideas,' he said.

As I recount this, I can feel the pull that existed to remedy the situation. But I wanted to make sure that my priority was to acknowledge the upset and being close, before we found a fix. When a practical fix did come about, I wanted the *connection* to take priority and the fix to become a less important, 'background' event.

Bids for practical fixes over relationship and connection can come in many different forms, including:

- Boredom: 'Dad, there's nothing to do, I'm bored.'
- Physical need: 'Can I have a plaster for this scratch?' 'I've got a tummy ache.'

- The need for things: 'I'm hungry.' 'Can I watch…?' 'Can you get me…?'

Although a parent's attempts to 'right' the difficulty through taking action can feel validating in some ways (and there will be times, of course, when you child is ACTUALLY hungry or in need of help!), it can also be confusing in a world where an overt focus on 'solutions' quickly becomes complicated and unworkable.

Focusing on the *connection* helps a child to lessen her concern to have the right thing, or to be entertained. Rather, she is able to connect more fully with the thing that really keeps her feeling safe and held, her relationship to you.

When a child's relationship to you is at the heart of things, her ability to cope with the many unfair and difficult things in the world has a more secure and fundamental solution. She doesn't need to ensure that she is fixed or entertained, or that everything is fair and equally distributed. Of course, she will care a bit, and finding a gentle solution doesn't necessarily overwhelm this balance, but your attempts to resettle her into connection and relationship with you provide a much more emotionally containing solution.

WHEN IT'S A STRUGGLE

'When you reconnect, one of the things that can happen – not always, but some of the time – is that you create something new. You figure out a way to do something together that you have never done before. If you create something new, you grow. And children are about growing.'
Ed Tronick, psychologist (Radio New Zealand interview, 2020)

A father told me a story of when his son was young. There had been some family upheavals and the son had taken to coming into his bed in the night. Feeling that his son needed this extra comfort he had let him climb in, but as the family situation settled, his son continued to want to sleep in with him and my friend just could not sleep. Eventually, after a couple of months, he decided that his son needed to stay in his own bed. Each night he took his son back to his bed only to find him returning within ten minutes. This went on through the night.

Finally, after a week of trying they were at a stand-off. Both father and son were sitting in the corridor, in the early hours of the morning, father refusing to let the son come into his bed and son refusing to return to his own. Feeling broken, he looked down at his son whose arms were crossed over his chest, his shoulders hunched and determined. The father felt tears well up in his eyes. His son looked up at him and swallowed hard.

'I love you, you know I do,' said the dad. 'But I can't sleep with you in the bed'.

His son put his head on his dad's arm and they slumped against each other.

'Can you give me an extra good cuddle and can I have your old bear?' asked his son. The dad got the old bear and took his son into the bedroom. They had a cuddle and his son fell asleep in his own bed for the first time in months.

When there is an acceptance of difficulty, limits and vulnerability, our emotional connection with our child, rather than dwindling, slowly becomes more expansive and engaged. Children watch us being open, honest and trying.

In a world of real ups and downs, connections and disconnections, your child will experience loving, gentle, soothing responses but also, harsh, quick, cross responses from you. She comes to recognize excited playful responses, stressed, rushed responses, distracted vague responses, confident responses, nervous responses and contradictory responses. In each of these interactions, her emotional understanding grows. She learns how emotions heighten, adapt and change. She experiences vulnerability, resilience and repairs.

Parents have a whole array of limits. Things they cannot do, times when they can't cope, emotions they find difficult to bear. In relationships these limits make themselves known. They come up to the surface. And yet, trying to push through these limits, to pretend they aren't there, somehow just makes things more uneasy and edgy. Sometimes, parents think their limits will damage their child; and they feel guilty or upset. The truth is that limits, thought about honestly, can motivate you and your child to find other ways to connect and relate. So, as in the example above, the father's inability to have his son sleeping in with him, meant that they had to think about other ways to manage the son's emotional needs. Rather than acting as a barrier, the father's need for his own space, when addressed honestly, gets worked through and can create new connections and emotional growth.

EXPRESS YOUR VULNERABILITY

Sometimes, the biggest thing that comes with being human and limited – and truthful about this – is the expression of vulnerability and need. A child can come to feel that her need for connection is very one-way. She concludes, 'I need my dad; he's busy.' 'I annoy him.' 'He has control over everything. I have none.' In this context, when a child knows that you care, that you are affected by her needs and how she feels, it can feel equalizing and reassuring.

Whenever parents and children get caught in a struggle, when the parent is open and clear about their emotional limits, but nonetheless creates space for the child to respond and communicate about this, something seems to change. Rather than seeing herself pitted against her parent, the child experiences the parent as *with* her, as jointly struggling and trying to work things through. When both you and your child have faced a problem sincerely and openly, a new sense of trust and understanding emerges. Whilst you have limits, your child feels assured that her needs will be valued and thought about, even if there isn't an obvious solution.

In this process there is no abrupt end point; rather, the relationship keeps moving and shifting to see how a range of needs might be balanced. Often this new connected sense comes about after a lot of trying to balance and shift and manage different demands. It seems to arrive when all the other options have been exhausted.

DON'T HIDE YOUR LIMITS

Although you might feel that your limits work *against* your child, handled sensitively, she can come to understand that limits shown with vulnerability and openness help newness and connection grow. She realizes that you are human, that you also experience big emotions and overwhelm and that everyone does. She sees that all relationships have limits, and this helps her understand her own struggles and difficulties.

Each difficulty, inadequacy and failure, when reflected on honestly, has the capacity to help your child learn and grow. Her emotional responses become more open and agile. She begins to understand the shifts and change in relationships and the realness of other people's capacities and limits.

Here are some of the things a child learns from our imperfections, limits and failures:

- She learns that to be human is to have emotional limits and that rather than having to hide these limits, she can express them and respect them.

- When she sees you being open about difficulties, she knows that it is okay to be vulnerable and that this realness and openness can invite connection.
- She discovers that she can recognize and acknowledge her mistakes, she can let things pass, she can see the funny and the wonky – and accept all of this.
- She learns to be kind to herself and to others.
- It becomes easier for her to be human too.

AIM FOR REALITY OVER PERFECTION

I'm a big fan of 'good enough' parenting (chapter 4). I enjoy the creative shifts and changes, blunders and opportunities in relationships. But relationships can also be very difficult. Sometimes the gaps are too big, the reconnections are too sparse and hard to achieve. There are times when a child's needs are not responded to in a good enough or timely manner. This could be for a brief period before things return to normal. At other times situations are long standing.

> My friend Obhi's mum was an alcoholic. When he was younger she would be drunk when he came home from school. He remembers her setting fire to the kitchen. Yelling at neighbours. Spending food money on wine which he was sent out to buy. Every now and then she would seek treatment and would be sober for a few months. He remembers her telling concerned social workers, 'The kids are fine. They've never done without. They don't really realize what's going on with me.'
>
> As he got older, he would challenge his mother more. The more he challenged, the more she seemed to fall apart. 'You're right', she'd acknowledge. 'I'm hopeless and useless. I just mess up again and again. You're better off without me. You've always been so strong. Nothing ever affects you.'

A few years ago, when Obhi had his first child, his mum came around. He was making tea in the kitchen but he could hear his mum talking to his wife through the door.

'It was very tough on the kids,' said his mum. 'I struggled with drink. I drank my way through whole years. I can't really remember much but I can remember Obhi having to cook for the other kids, wash the clothes and hide my money so he could get food. I don't know how he got through. It meant he didn't get many opportunities. A lot of the time he didn't get to school because I was so bad.'

Obhi listened from the kitchen, frozen. It was the first time his mother had ever acknowledged the hardship, loneliness and neglect he had experienced without either becoming angry and defensive or turning the attention back to her needs. Hearing his mother describe his childhood in this honest, straightforward way made him feel sane for the first time in his life.

For a long while Obhi replayed this conversation with his wife and friends. Each time, he felt he was letting go of some of the hurt and confusion and disappointment that had constantly haunted him. 'I thought about my baby daughter, and how, if we ever let her down in any way I would always try to be straight and truthful with her. I would always try to understand her experience and acknowledge it.'

Obhi's experience was extreme, and it was upsetting. He had a grandfather who managed to care for him and his siblings for some of the time and Obhi was a bright, intelligent boy – but it had nonetheless been hard for him to understand and manage. For many years he felt it affected his sense of self and his experiences. His partner had helped him reflect over the years, but his mother's acknowledgement created a big shift.

Although most families and children don't experience anything near to Obhi's situation, we all have a basic human need to have our emotional experiences honestly recognized. For children, this is particularly marked. A child has little other experience of life and is dependent on her adult. She is therefore far more likely to blame herself or become ashamed and confused by difficulties. Having even very small emotional difficulties acknowledged assists her in understanding that she isn't at fault, that she has nothing to be ashamed of.

Essentially, rather than weakening her love or sense or respect for you, seeing that you can talk about and recognize what happened increases her sense of orientation, confidence and safety. She comes to know that being human is full of messy contradictions, complications and opportunities – and that that is okay.

American child psychologist Mary Main has carried out extensive research into emotional security and attachments (the ability to form stable, loving relationships) in adulthood. Her findings speak to Obhi's experience. She suggests that the long-term picture for children in terms of their emotional processing may not so much rest on having consistently 'happy' or uncomplicated childhood experiences. Rather, she found that over time, the ability to talk about experiences reflectively and coherently was a very strong indicator of emotional health and competency, particularly when their experiences had been difficult. Whilst this in no way neutralizes Obhi's experiences (a child in his situation would need more than acknowledgement of the difficulties), it is an important reminder for us all, over the difficulties and complications of family life.

As a psychologist, I have also seen the positive impact on parents of openly acknowledging their behaviour – and their own emotions. It seems to clarify their purpose, settle their intentions and help them let go of self-blame and guilt; instead, they are able to focus on making positive changes.

'Openly acknowledging' behaviour means describing what happened without blaming others, becoming defensive or minimizing the impact. For example, if you became angry that morning when you were interrupted on a work project, you might say, '*I got really angry when I was working earlier. I shouted and it was too loud and when you wanted to talk, I said "not now" in a sharp, harsh way. It took me a long time to stop feeling cross and you felt frightened. I am sorry.*'

Of course, it's always helpful to then make a plan. For example, '*Next time when I feel rushed and pressured in my work I'll make sure you know how long I'm going to be and we'll think of some things you can do.*' But the important thing is to start by acknowledging, coherently, emotionally difficult situations.

When Main describes the need to talk about experiences 'coherently', she is referring to the ability to consider and reflect upon the good and bad, the loving and the rejecting experiences a person has had, with a sense of perspective and nuance. Needs and losses, disappointments, expectations and failures need to all be taken into account.

This ability to recognize that relationships are emotionally complex and contradictory, loving and difficult, upsetting and supportive helped those in Main's study to navigate and work through emotional difficulties in other later relationships. With a coherent understanding, adults were able to recognize and openly reflect on difficulties. They were able to trust that relationships can be robust and honest and truthful.

TALK ABOUT THE HARD STUFF

Although Main's research involved adults who had had significant difficulties, it's important to open up conversations that acknowledge the realities of your relationships with your child at many different levels – both large and small. It's often easiest to begin talking about general behaviours as a family. You might say, *'You know how Mummy was really sad and a bit teary after getting some bad news from Granny?'* or *'Do you remember when I got shouty this morning about the games on the floor and how I stood on that piece?'* When you do this, it invites children in to discuss what happened. They have a voice and can give you feedback.

Here are some of the things that help encourage honesty and openness in conversations with children:

HAVE A 'YES, THAT MAKES SENSE' ATTITUDE

When your child speaks about her experience, it's important that this is met with openness and a 'Yes, that makes sense' attitude. This validates her feelings and gives her the confidence to be vulnerable and open. Sometimes this means that you have to actively try to get into your child's headspace. Here are some examples of what I mean by a 'Yes, that makes sense' attitude:

> Child: *'You said, "You have to go to Simrita's" and I didn't want to and you just said goodbye and then you went and left me.'*
> Adult: *'I can see that it felt like I went quickly, and you were not ready...'*
> Child: *'Yes – I didn't know you were going to say goodbye that fast.'*
> Adult: *'So you didn't know what was happening and it left you feeling worried or not sure?'*
> Child: *'It made me feel like crying but I had to pretend to be happy because Simrita's mum was there.'*
> Adult: *'Yes, that makes sense, so you were trying to be okay for Simrita's mum but felt upset inside.'*
> Child: *'Yes.'*

The temptation here can be to want to come in with a *'but...'* in an effort to get your child to see the 'reality' of situations, to acknowledge her part in the frustration or simply to justify your actions in your mind. Hold back on this. Your child is doing an important thing. She is learning how to express things through words and developing trust in your ability to listen and understand. Rather than an exchange of blame, or increased avoidance, when you allow and make space for her experiences, something different happens. You connect with her and the wider context can more easily begin to unfold.

DETAILS ARE GOOD

As she gets older your child will be able to give you more detail. Again, in developing coherent understandings, this is really helpful and important. As she explains the nuances, she is orientating her emotional response more fully and your acknowledgement of these helps her system to step down. She can see more clearly where her emotions come from and gains more perspective:

> Child: 'I hate the music you listen to on the radio.'
> Parent: 'What bothers you about it?'
> Child: 'It's so boring. It makes me feel bored as soon as you turn it on.'
> Parent: 'Can you think of why? Does it remind you of something?'
> Child: 'It reminds me of Sunday afternoons when there's nothing to do and you and Dad just read the papers.'
> Parent: 'Yes, we did have a lot of very quiet Sundays when my knee was bad. Tell me more about the feeling on those Sundays...'

Over time, as these conversations evolve, if I feel that a child is comfortable and has been fully heard, I sometimes add my experience. But only if I don't feel hot or defensive or annoyed. At first the great majority of the conversation is focused on the situation from the child's point of view. You job is to be open, to understand and witness. To resist quick fixes but slowly think about what can be changed and what can't. To reconnect.

The thing about emotional intelligence is that it is adaptive and capable and nuanced. When relationships are reflected on with honesty, care and compassion, and when that reflection helps future interactions to become easier and more responsive, then a child's emotional intelligence is strengthened. It becomes larger, more agile and more adaptive.

POINTS TO REMEMBER

- **Your relationship with your child is the place where she learns about and works through emotions**.
- **As your child grows older, many things can interrupt this emotional connection**. Perhaps she learns that she needs to be more independent, or it might be that frustrations and limitations in the relationships block her sense of trust and security.
- **It's important that your emotional connection to your child develops and grows through these gaps or difficulties**. This is where **bids and repairs and reconnections** come in.
  - **Bids** are the efforts your child makes to emotionally connect to you. Her bids will often be clumsy and awkward; but with your support, she gets more confident and capable in making these bids.
  - **Repairs and reconnections** happen when you are real about your limits and when you take the time to acknowledge and understand the times your child has had difficulty or has felt a lack of connection to you.
- **When you can acknowledge and work through difficulties, limits and problems, your emotional connection with our child slowly becomes more resilient, more expansive and more engaged**.
- **Your child watches you being open and honest**. She trusts that she can bring all of her emotions and experiences to you and that you will work hard to connect with her.

PART TWO

FIVE STEPS TO EQ

6

EMOTIONAL GROWTH
THROUGH THE FIVE STEPS

In Part One we looked in detail at how your child's emotions work, and why their connection with you is so important. In this part of the book we will explore five things you can focus on to nurture your child's emotional intelligence and help ease difficult emotions.

So, why five steps? Well, in the modern world emotions can seem complex and difficult. The emotions a child struggles with come to seem so much more than emotions. They can seem to be a sign that a child is broken and 'wrong'. A parent's job in managing and sorting these emotions becomes large and, frankly, scary. We try to help our children become 'less'. Less angry, less sad, less distracted, less argumentative. Although we try to listen, understand and help a child express his emotions, the underlying focus is on the ways in which we can avoid, reduce and get rid of these.

But emotions have been designed to help your child respond to the world. Focusing on pushing away or reducing her emotions, over and above opening them out and helping him to understand them, can make things tight and nervous – and often cause explosions of pent-up emotions.

The process of trying to *move through* emotions whilst at the same time trying to *avoid* them reminds me of swimming using doggy paddle. When you swim using doggy paddle, you're essentially trying to get through the water but also working desperately hard to try and keep the water away. Doggy paddle isn't particularly effective or pleasurable. In fact, it's choppy and hard. If you and your child were to swim in this way, you might at any point go under, gulping and choking and generally have quite a difficult, miserable time.

This all changes when you learn that you can put your face down into the water. The funny things is that having your face in the water doesn't feel like you're drowning. In fact, it feels easy and peaceful and agile and light. There's so much to see and you can move *oh so* freely.

This is what it's like with your child's emotions. You start out thinking you need to somehow rescue him from his emotions. You prepare to thrash around, struggling against these emotions. It's intense and exhausting and frightening. And then somehow you realize you can *lean into* the emotions. When you do, you notice that they are so much easier and more fluid than you had imagined.

You no longer try to pull your child away with avoidance and blind effort. Suddenly you're both immersed. The struggle stops. With the emotions there, all around, you can see and understand and think. It feels natural and restorative and full of opportunities. This doesn't mean that you accept all behaviours (Step 5 explains how to manage behaviours that draw attention away from vulnerable emotions), but it does mean emotional intelligence becomes much more pleasurable and even (shock horror) fun (see Step 4 for many examples of this!).

In short, these five steps aim to help recover a sense of comfort and confidence in emotions – for both you and your child. After all, these emotions are the tools your child will use to get to know the world and interact with others. They will help him, so they need to be tuned into and opened out. And you may find that emotions that perhaps in the past you shied away from or tried to quash are now seen in a different, more understandable light.

All five steps focus on the relationship between you and your child because this is where his emotions get experienced, opened out and worked through. This is where your approach can make a difference.

STEP 1 takes a look at how to **Aim for Simplicity**. Emotions can become surrounded by complexity and complicated understandings which tie you and your child up in knots, increasing struggle and unease. This step looks at how your child's emotions steadily develop and grow when treated with simplicity and ease.

STEP 2 focuses on the need to **Encourage Acceptance**. Stepping away from fighting or stigmatizing emotions means that they become much easier to be around. When all emotions are given their time they bring a depth, warmth and energy to experiences.

STEP 3 shows why it's important to **Respond with Compassion**. Whilst emotional intelligence develops through opening out and leaning-in to emotions, some emotions can become large and stuck and anxious. This step thinks about how you can help your child shift anxious fear and avoidance, becoming more aware of his resourceful and courageous emotions.

STEP 4 is about how to **Increase Playfulness** (which might surprise you!). Emotional intelligence happens best when there is a sense of exuberance and welcome around emotions. Playfulness provides the perfect way in. In this step we consider how your relationship to your child can become livelier and more animated and how, in response, his emotions open out, becoming hopeful and expressive.

STEP 5 shows you skills to **'Contain' and Connect** to the emotions that push others away. As we discussed in Part One, sometimes your child's open, vulnerable emotions get overtaken by defensive emotions and behaviours which block understanding and connection. These defensive emotions seek quick solutions and push others away hard and fast. Step 5 focuses on ways in which you can help slow your child's emotions down and bring him back into connection. This will include thinking about how you can place limits on behaviour and how you can steady and strengthen the emotional connection between you.

Each chapter begins by introducing that step, unpacking what it brings to your child and explaining its link to emotional intelligence. The second part of the chapter shows you how to put this step into practice in your day-to-day interactions with your child. It looks at the key skills that you can build and gives examples of conversations relating to this step. Each step ends with '5 Points to Remember' with key take-aways of the step for busy parents.

7

STEP 1:
AIM FOR SIMPLICITY

'Sometimes the questions are complicated and the answers are simple.'
Dr Seuss

Step 1 looks at nurturing and making space for a child's developing EQ in a complicated, pressurized world. We look at how you can create a space away from complex ideas, anxiety and rush; and instead, support your child to develop his own more attuned, gradual understandings and expertise.

Joe and Laurie are playing. 'Joe, it's your turn.' says Laurie, stepping out of the shabby, slightly broken red play car.

'Brill!' says Joe, climbing in. 'Reversing, reversing,' he calls out. He has his arm along the passenger seat and frowns as he steers the car carefully backward. 'Parked!' he announces. 'Your turn, Laurie.'

This game has been going on for weeks. I often sit near and watch. They are completely immersed. Both have 'difficult' backgrounds. Joe has some learning disabilities and Laurie's home situation is very unsettled. His confidence is low and in some situations he is withdrawn. They are in different classes, two years apart, but have found each other out here in the playground.

The school are concerned and started to talk about separating the boys.

'What are you worried about?' I ask one teacher.

'I not sure, Anne,' she replies. 'This parking thing Joe does with Laurie is very safe and repetitive. It's like he's using it to avoid making real friends. I suppose I'm worried he's going to be left behind.'

Children are definitely quirky. Their sense of the world is slower, more offbeat. They dream, they play around, they live in fantasy worlds. As I rush out the door, one of mine will stop, look into the air wistfully and begin telling me in elaborate detail the plot line from a book or a TV programme.

And their interests… From the repetitiveness of a favourite story read nightly, to a fondness for the same comfy clothes, pockets full of stones and every kind of stick dragged back to the house. Hours spent fiddling around with toothpaste and soap in the bathroom. The desperation to buy one more moth-eaten, old cuddly toy from the school fair, to add to the pile on their bed. The collection of found objects in their drawers. They are fiddling, busy, squirrelly and slow.

In many ways children are removed from the adult world of complications, expectations, pressures and demands. This space allows a child the time to learn about the small and local, to develop the skills and abilities he will need, but also the emotional capacity, the sense of balance and steadiness. A child needs to have a confidence in managing himself before he can take on the complexity and demands of the bigger, wider world.

AN ATMOSPHERE OF COMPLICATION, WORRY AND INTERRUPTION

A child's parents are the main way in which he becomes introduced to the world. Ideally, they act to temper and balance the world and its busy, pushy, noisiness. Most parents understand this; they hope to keep life simple. When asked what they want for their child, they would probably say that they want him to be happy, kind, generous, to have good relationships, to be confident, to fulfil his potential.

However, whilst parents want to filter out the excess noise and demands, anxieties and pressures can creep in. Your attention can be drawn to a child's struggle to fit in or to make progress at school, or simply to manage his emotions in this busy, hectic world. You feel you should help. You might find yourself wondering how much you should be protecting your child and how much you should be helping him to adapt. Should you push him to achieve more? Perhaps you worry about his emotional capacity and his tendency to pull away.

The difficulty is that the more you worry about a child's capacity, the quicker and more reactive your responses can be. From a base of anxiety, you may find yourself:

- Seeing his emotional responses as complicated, different or signs of weakness.
- Jumping in to correct him.
- Pushing a child through a difficulty rather than focusing on his pace and capacity.
- Distracting, amusing or occupying a child to protect him from low-level emotional discomfort.
- Focusing on your child's academic or performance skills to give him a more secure footing in the world.

These interventions create complications for a child. The more his preferences, actions and thoughts are interrupted, the more he loses confidence in his ability to make sense of the world and try things out. Slowly he learns to see the world as a complex, difficult place and to look to other people's judgements and approval. For example, a child in this situation might wonder: 'Does my father think I am good enough?' 'Am I fitting in?' 'Is my teacher happy with my choices?' 'Am I doing better than X, Y, Z person?'

This process of looking outward can leave a child with less of a sense of his own capacities and preferences. He might find himself caught in trying to push himself harder and faster; or he might pull away, feeling overwhelmed and lost. His ability to develop his own simple, slow emotional responses becomes blocked or strained.

RESPONDING WITH SIMPLICITY

SLOW, SIMPLE AND ROOTED IN RELATIONSHIPS

I have not always been a fan of simplicity. In the past, I imagined that being simple was the same as being inactive or avoidant. I thought of it not savvy or adept enough. Perhaps, if I am honest, I thought it couldn't equip a child for the world. But slowly I am coming to understand that simplicity is not insubstantial. It is not passively standing by as a parent, leaving a child to move further and further from the real world.

Rather, simplicity allows a child to bring all of his curiosity and abilities to a situation. It supports his efforts to build up emotional resources and allows him the time to do this. A simple slow focus increases a parent's ability to recognize their child's actual needs. It allows him to climb his own mountain of development, rather than the mountains we keep noticing further down the line.

When you as a parent step outside of this anxiety, you become aware of the many quiet ways in which your child is shifting and learning. I saw this as I observed Joe and Laurie:

I remember clearly noticing all of the things that were happening around this parking game. Although their teacher worried that their play was avoidant and repetitive, the more I watched, the more I could see that they were very engaged and active.

Let me give you some examples:

One day a boy came over to their patch of playground to retrieve a ball. As he walked away he shouted back, 'You dumbos!' at the two boys.

'Don't listen to him, Joe,' said Laurie. 'He's always like that.'

'Oh yeah, I know,' said Joe nodding sagely.

With their protective seal reformed they could return to their play.

I also noticed an increasing amount of detail and role play. For example, the boys were interested in what it would be like to be experienced and capable; how their skills could help them respond and act in the world:

'My car's big and hard to move properly. You have to really know how to drive it,' said Joe, masterfully.

Or on another occasion, Joe commented: 'Sometimes I do this in building sites, you know, with big diggers and things like that.'

And then there was their own growing abilities to share experiences:

Laurie: 'My mum had to come in to talk to Miss yesterday because of my reading.'

Joe: 'Yeah – we have to practise it all the time in my class.'

WHAT WE CAN'T SEE – A CHILD'S ROOT GROWTH

My sister teaches four- to five-year-olds. She tells a story about a little boy in her class. The class were discussing the seasons and had put some bulbs into earth and then into the dark cupboard. 'Why do you think we put these bulbs into a dark place to start growing?' she asked the class.

A little boy put his hand up: 'Because they're shy?' he suggested.

This story makes me smile. In fact, he wasn't far off the mark. In the dark, a bulb's energy and effort goes into growing roots before the top growth starts to be stimulated by light. If the bulb is brought into the light before the roots are established, then the flower begins to push up before there is sufficient root support. Without enough roots, the flowers are small, feeble and stubby.

As with the bulb, a child's emotional roots need to mature to support his growth and development. Sometimes when we look in at our child's life, we mistakenly worry that he is not learning or developing enough. What we often miss is the quiet ways in which a child, once settled, will explore and experiment and find ways of steadying himself and establishing his roots. Too much intervention or distraction, anxiety and pressure can interrupt this slower, simpler root growth.

A PARENT'S ROLE IN CULTIVATING SIMPLICITY

When I speak about the process of root growth, I don't mean to imply that a child isn't in need of our support. He is. A child needs his adults to help him in many ways:

- To feel safe and secure. Joe and Laurie used their relationship to provide a sense of comfort and protection. A child might do this through siblings, friends or teachers, but the primary person he does this through is you, his parent. You provide that background sense that all is right, that you have confidence in his actions and abilities, that he is loved and cared for.

- To allow him to be ordinary, fallible and human. A child's development can be very esoteric. He doesn't progress in a straight line; rather he has periods of learning, periods of obvious change and development and times of quietness and consolidation. He therefore naturally follows his own pace and interests developing his own individual tempo. He needs this process to be nurtured rather than corrected or criticized.

- To support him in developing a kind and open relationship with his emotional responses. When a child has the opportunity to respond to a variety of situations and emotions without either being pushed, full throttle, forward, or being 'saved' from any discomfort or worry, then he begins to feel grounded and steady and competent. This means he gets to say he is bored, without anyone telling him that he couldn't possibly be, or responding by finding a quick 'fix'. He gets to say that he doesn't like a friend without being told that he should be kinder. He is able to sit in the sandpit raking his hands through the sand and not be prompted to make something or challenge himself more.

- To bring a gentle, unhurried, unworried focus. A child's emotions work best when they are slow. He inevitably picks up on the busyness and distractions all around. When he is helped to settle and become comfortable, he has the energy to focus his efforts and work with his emotions more effectively.

WHY SIMPLICITY IS GOOD FOR EQ

SIMPLE EMOTIONS ARE SLOWER, MORE RESPONSIVE AND LESS REACTIVE

When your child's life is based on simpler understandings and relationships, his emotions are slower and more attuned. He is more perceptive, noticing and enjoying more. He can take his time developing his understandings and explorations.

Although he will experience many fast, hot, anxious emotions, simplicity allows him to then steady and regulate these. He is more able to shift his pace, slow down and orientate himself, developing and adapting his responses.

SIMPLICITY BUILDS UP EMOTIONAL CAPACITY, NOT JUST ABILITY

A simple approach recognizes that the complicated, pressured pace of the world can overwhelm a child. When you focus on simplifying things for your child you help create space away from complicated demands and ideas. You support him to develop and steady his responses around smaller, simpler situations so that he slowly builds up his emotional capacity. Gradually, your child learns to seek out this space to recuperate and recharge. He knows that he can find you and that you will help.

SIMPLICITY IS HONEST AND TRUTHFUL

Simple understandings are honest and kind. Being human means becoming reconciled with being ordinary, vulnerable, sometimes foolish and silly, and often needing support. Learning this is part of emotional intelligence. When your child falls short of what is expected, when he makes mistakes, when he is unkind or unhelpful, he knows that you will see past these mistakes to his goodness and worth. In this way, his sense of himself becomes wider than his mistakes. He learns to see limitations as normal and human, both in himself and others. He discovers that he can repair situations and rebuild relationships through openness and honesty.

YOUR CHILD DOESN'T FEEL THE NEED TO RUSH THROUGH THE WORLD

Whilst your child naturally wants to fit in with others and respond with excitement to the world, over time he balances his efforts with a growing sense of his own preferences, values and capacity. With your help, he recognizes that he doesn't always need to respond or keep up. He learns that he can stand back, taking a slower, quieter pace.

HOW TO AIM FOR SIMPLICITY: KEY SKILLS

In a book about emotional intelligence it's easy to think that helping a child analyse emotions will allow her to become more emotionally intelligent. Unfortunately, when we step in to help our child think, we can bring in our own complicated understandings and preoccupations. When we aim for simplicity, we give him a sense of our emotional presence and support so that he can decide what's important and what isn't.

STEP AWAY FROM ANALYSING SITUATIONS

Imagine your child's friend has a birthday party and doesn't invite him. It's one of his best friends. You feel hurt and upset. Rather than leave him to bottle up his emotions, you want to let him know that you love him, that he can share his worries and that the party doesn't matter.

So you try asking gently: '*Are you feeling sad that Nidha didn't invite you to her party?*'

Perhaps he shakes his head. '*I don't want to go to the party.*'

'*It's okay to feel upset when someone doesn't invite you to their party,*' you say.

'*I'm not upset, and I don't care about Nidha!*' he blurts out, his voice wavering and tears shining in his eyes.

Or maybe he simply says: '*Yeah, I know,*' without going any further.

Although you might assume that prompting a child about something you suspect has been upsetting him is a good way of saying '*it's okay to talk, you're okay, the situation's okay,*' it can jump a child forward, inviting him into worrying or overthinking situations. Your comment serves to draw his attention to something which he may have already let go of or over which he has very little control. He feels unsettled and defensive.

When we take a simple approach, we want to create a sense of ease and clarity.

For a child's hurt to be resolved, he doesn't need to work through the reason for his pain. He needs something far more fundamental. He needs to know that he's loved, that he is wanted and that he's safe and protected. When he has this sense of security, he is able to decide how he feels about situations and what he needs.

Allowing Him to Set the Pace

Responding to your child with simplicity means connecting with your child, allowing him to decide what he thinks and what he is concerned about. You stay with him, rather than moving ahead. Here are some of the ways in which you can 'simplify' and let him set the pace:

- A child is far more likely to open up about uncertainty and difficulty when he feels secure in your support and love. Instead of prompting him, spend plenty of time connecting with him and being clear about your love and enjoyment of his company.
- If he is carrying a weight of sadness or confusion, your kind and warm presence will reassure him that he can let down his guard and rest into you. He might say: *'Can I sit on your lap?'*, *'I feel a bit sad'*, or he might put things into words: *'I don't like Nidha because she didn't invite me to her party.'*
- A simple approach means responding with gentleness and ease. Your job is to stay right by his side. Not rushing ahead or reacting with more energy than he is. You might simply say: *'You're thinking about Nidha and the party and feeling sad.'*
- You might just softly rub his back or stroke his hair or put a hand lightly on his shoulders.

- Allowing this situation to 'simply be' means not seeking to verbally reassure him (e.g. *'There will be other parties'*, or *'You will have a bigger party'*), not trying to move him through his feelings (by telling him that he doesn't need to be upset), and not analysing the situation (*'It could be that her parents got confused…'*). Rather, the simple focus is on helping your child feel held and loved.

Complicated ideas take a child away from a sense of security and wellbeing and hook him into worries and problems. When you move toward comforting a child and away from analysis and detailed understandings, you teach your child how to let go of worries and rumination whilst finding the comfort and security to settle herself.

WELCOME MILD DISCOMFORT

Whilst some emotions can be tight and knotted, a lot more emotions are just mildly uncomfortable. A child needs to experience a lot of uncomfortable emotions for him to be able to differentiate between those that are real problems and those that he can let go of. And the best way to learn to be with uncomfortable emotions is against a backdrop of ease and simplicity.

Oliver Burkeman calls the ability to tolerate mildly uncomfortable emotions a superpower. Why? Because through automatically pulling away from mild discomfort, human beings avoid making new friends, learning skills, exploring, resting and repairing. When you support your child through mild discomfort, he learns that the feeling rises and falls, that it is uncomfortable but not worrying. He recognizes that he can do what he needs to do and that this feeling is not a signal to stop. He becomes more motivated and assured.

So, what does mild discomfort look like? Mild discomfort is an itchy emotion. It can feel like irritability, boredom, low-level anxiety, like the need for a snack, the need to be distracted, to have screen time.

When we try to sort out a child's mild discomfort with distraction (for example by giving a child something to eat, putting him on a screen, or buying a new toy), we temporarily pause the feeling; but as soon as the distraction finishes, the feeling returns. A child that is distracted whenever they are anxious or irritable starts to override his natural instinct to seek human company and support. Rather than helping him process the emotion, the distraction pushes it to the background. When the distraction finishes either the problematic emotion returns or they have missed an opportunity to learn how to queue, or have their hair cut, or look out the window for a 30-minute car journey.

How to Help Your Child Move Through Mild Discomfort:

- As a general rule, hold back from responding to his uncomfortable feelings with distractions or fixing. Instead, show him that you recognize his discomfort, listen and slow your reactions.
- *Expect* that your child can wait in queues with you, go on short car journeys, sit at the hairdressers without needing the diversion of a screen, or a snack or a bribe.
- See if he can have a think about what people are doing when they aren't looking at phones. How do they do it? Ask him how he waits when he's in school.
- If it feels like he will struggle, start small. See if he is able to wait for five minutes with you. Tell him that you are both going to see what it feels like to wait. Help him to listen to the noises all around, tuning in to his breath, noticing all the feelings that come up. These feelings might itch or worry him, they might feel heavy and frustrated, or they might feel open and curious. You can ask him which ones

come up. When he tells you, don't try to analyse or fix them, just acknowledge their presence.

- Observe with him that feelings move through us all of the time; that sometimes they are comfortable and easy and at other time they are difficult and distracting. It can be useful to describe them as waves that move in, intensify and then fade away without us having to do anything or change anything.
- Make time to sit quietly with him on a park bench or lie with him in the garden looking at the sky. Allow him to put his hand on your stomach so you can show him how to deepen and steady his breath.
- If he gets irritable around things like writing, drawing, or practising an instrument, don't step in to either argue with him or reduce the demand. Slow things down.
- Sit near to him, listen to his discomfort, clarify and let him know you understand, then gently bring him back to what he was doing. He might discover that approaching something more slowly helps him to feel more relaxed without feeling he has to step away straight away. Prompt him gently, asking what he was hoping for when he started and how he could achieve just a bit of this before he finishes.

DEVELOP SIMPLER UNDERSTANDINGS OF DIFFICULT EMOTIONS

Some years ago I worked with a ten-year-old girl called Malia. When the referral came through, our department secretary brought me five large stuffed files, held together with elastic bands. They were full of complex assessments. This young girl had been assessed for attention difficulties, demand avoidance, sensory processing problems as well as an autistic spectrum diagnosis and eating difficulties.

The reason that Malia came to see me was because of her anxiety around social situations. The sense of being overwhelmed when others were around was preventing her from attending school, from seeing family members and from going out at the weekends. Her parents were desperate to help her make sense of her experiences.

We worked on this for a long time together. Eventually, in one session Malia told me that she remembered a health worker telling her mother that as soon as she had heard Malia talking it had been an obvious sign that she was 'on the spectrum' (autistic spectrum).

'I felt like everyone else could see into me. That they could spot right away that I was different,' Malia said. She felt exposed and ashamed and confused.

I wanted things to be simpler for Malia. I wanted her to have her own understandings and judgements and to take away her sense of being scrutinised and strange, so we spoke about the things that could make a voice sound different. I asked her to record herself talking when she was walking down the street, when she was with me and when she was on her own, talking to her cat who she loved dearly. When we listened to the recordings we noticed that her voice really varied depending on where she was, and how exposed/relaxed she was.

'No one can see or listen in to you and know what sort of person you are,' I told her. 'And even if they could, you are constantly rewriting yourself and changing.'

Malia thought about this for a while. 'I always thought that my voice was strange and weird and that some bit of me inside was like that too.'

Although Malia's difficulties were significant, the feeling that others were scrutinizing and sensing something 'in her' that she was somehow not able to perceive herself only acted to exacerbate this. It created a sense of distance and threat between her and others, tightening her anxiety and aloneness.

Understandings that are complicated and which create a feeling of being different or unusual can leave a child feeling scrutinized, judged and excluded.

To be able to make sense of his experiences and abilities, a child needs kind and generous explanations based in a trust that his actions make sense. He needs explanations that celebrate idiosyncrasies and quirks, that highlight his efforts, his humanity and his goodness.

The process of helping a child to identify simpler, gentler understandings doesn't mean denying the impact of a difficulty. Rather, it makes clear that the difficulty is common to others but has become pressurized and difficult to manage.

A NOTE ABOUT DIAGNOSIS

When a child's difficulties have become significant and difficult to manage, he might have heard them described in terms of specific diagnoses. Although I have seen children with very severe problems, I have never seen a child where we couldn't make sense of his difficulties in more simple, human terms.

Diagnoses collect together patterns of behaviours that we can all see, rather than signs that seem invisible or under the surface. Complicated explanations, often attached to diagnoses, particularly those suggesting 'inherent' difficulties relating to brain functioning, are normally both impossible to know for sure, particularly in individual children, and to varying degrees they can also create a sense of disconnection and feelings of brokenness or weakness that push a child away.

I'm not suggesting that diagnoses are all bad or shouldn't be used. Instead, I think it's important that children understand the diagnosis is there mainly to help professionals organize and sort out help.

Seeing Through the Problem – Back to the Person

There is a tendency for a child's difficult, fast emotions to dominate his understanding of himself. Although it's important that you help him manage the hot, quick emotions through acknowledging and containing his experience, the emotions that you want your child to begin becoming more familiar with are the simpler, slower, more vulnerable emotions. These emotions have more perspective. They are more open and balanced.

This happens best *out* of the heat of the moment. For example, if he had been acting in a demanding or aggressive way earlier in the day you might later ask, '*Can you remember what your feelings were about? Were you feeling left out or cross or frustrated? Can you see if you can explain that frustration more to me?*'

If your child had been cruel or unkind you might later talk with him about whether he also noticed feeling nervous or upset. He might only notice that he felt tight and angry. That's fine – your role is to support him in thinking about his reactions more widely and with more kindness.

This process of looking for the gentler, softer, more open explanations, makes it possible for your child to relax and think more. He connects with his own understandings and experiences and becomes more able to navigate and regulate his responses. Most importantly he trusts that he makes sense, that he is a good person, that he is worthwhile and loveable.

HELPING YOUR CHILD TO SIMPLIFY HIS OWN EXPERIENCES

When a child's emotional difficulties are understood as complex and serious, he becomes distanced from his own experiences.

It's important to help him simplify his experiences so that he becomes more connected and capable around his emotions.

To help highlight his own simpler understandings and experiences you might ask:

- When do the difficulties you have make it harder to do things? When is it easier?
- What happens to the difficulties when you feel rushed, embarrassed, pressured?
- How do you become more comfortable with this difficulty? Are there times when it worries you less? When you feel more confident in your abilities?

Acknowledging When a Child is Less than his Best Self, but not Making it a Big Deal

For your child, seeing beyond his daily difficulties is helped when the adults around a child are prepared to share their less-than-good behaviours and faults. We reflect that we can be unfair and unkind, moody and difficult, but also funny, loving and generous.

This happens best in conversations. You might say: '*I was really grumpy that afternoon. I am sorry.*' Or '*I kept looking at the hoover, lying on the ground, hoping Daddy would pick it up and use it!*'

In my family we often laugh at our quirks: '*Do you remember when I broke Nana's cup and I felt so guilty that I pretended* to still drink out of it even with the tea leaking out?' Or 'I was just thinking about the time when I got really cranky about X, and then Mummy burped and we all couldn't stop laughing.' Children learn that emotions come and go, that underneath we are safe and kind and good enough. That our foibles are human and can bring others closer.

Over time children pick up on these non-complicated understandings. They begin to bring a kindness and understanding to their own experiences. Sometimes recalling them with humour; sometimes sharing these experiences in a spirit of generosity to help another out with their difficulties.

DEALING WITH AN OVERWHELMING WORLD

Whilst a child is learning about his own emotional responses and the actions and feelings of those around him, he is also trying to understand about the world. When I was a child I remember worrying about nuclear war and famine. The children I see today worry about the environment, political uncertainty, racism, poverty and war (and, at the time of writing, the COVID-19 pandemic).

The problem is that these issues are so complex and deep-rooted that children easily become fearful and panicked. It's important that we help a child to find a base of simplicity and safety through which he can slowly and gradually understand these issues, engaging with them as he feels more ready and capable.

When a child feels overwhelmed, he needs to feel your steady presence and to know that it's okay to let you take the weight of the worry. Let me give you an example:

It's the evening. Your child has been learning about the environment at school. As you're tidying up, he comes to you panicky and upset:

'Daddy, I am worried about what we will do when temperatures go up and the world begins to flood.'

'Gosh you're thinking about a lot. Tell me a little bit more.' (You stop and move closer to show him that you're properly listening.)

'Mrs McKenzie said that the sea levels will go up and we will get really bad weather and the polar bears won't have a home because the ice will melt.'

'Yes, I hear you.' (Pause.) 'You're learning about the environment and now all of those thoughts and worries are going around and around in your head.'

'But, Daddy, I don't want it all to happen!'

'I can see that. Let me sit by you so you can lean in near to me.'

You might then say: 'Some things are so big for us to hold in our small bodies. Where are you feeling it all?'

'I can't breathe, Daddy, and I keep thinking about it all the time.'

'So it's up here?' (Put your hand on his chest.)

'Yes, but it's also in my tummy and then in my head again.'

'Let me see if I can help you manage that big worry. Let's try and help bring that thinking in. Can you hear my breathing?' (Breath out slowly.) 'Listen to my breath coming out...'

(Child sits quietly and listens.)

'Have a go breathing with me, like this.' (Focus on belly breathing, extending your outbreath.)

Wait a little bit. Give him time to listen and breathe with you.

When his breathing slows down you can say: 'You and me, here now, are safe. We're sitting in the kitchen and the cat's scratching his ear. I'm clearing up after dinner and you're safe here with me.' (Bringing him into the now.)

As with all anxiety and worry, your job is to give him a sense of safety and security.

HELPING YOUR CHILD WHEN HE FEELS OVERWHELMED

As your child grows, he becomes more aware of the world around him, environmental disasters, wars and famines. Helping him ground his emotions enables him to step back and cope when he becomes overwhelmed. You can:

- **Support him whilst he explains**. Ask minimal questions but let him know you have time to hear it. You might say 'uh-huh', 'I can see', 'mmm'.
- **Help take the weight from him**. 'Such a lot that you're carrying. Let Daddy carry some of that for you. Did you know that's what daddies and mummies are for? They carry these things for you, so that you can do small things and make small changes without feeling everything and getting overloaded.'
- **Bring him back into the now**. Help him locate the overload in his body. Bring attention to that area and breathe out, pause, then slowly breathe in again. When you see that his breathing has settled, you can orientate him to his surroundings and the normality of home life. You might say, 'Let's make a cup of tea,' or 'Sit here next to me whilst I peel the carrots.' Then slowly talk about the here-and-now. 'I've got some pizza dough proving for later', 'Grandad rang, he says he's got three new jumpers.' Keep conversations normal and everyday and orientated and bring in everyday routines and gentle tasks.

Reducing Overwhelm

A child's desire to understand and fit in with the world is natural and good, but it can be overwhelming as he absorbs all of its pressure and complication.

It's very important for your child to learn about the complexities of the world from a base of simplicity and calm. You want to ensure that he develops his capacity to tolerate frightening and confusing information slowly and steadily. When a child is taking in too much, too quickly, he becomes panicky, worry takes over and he feels confused.

Here is some of the advice I give to parents when their children are struggling with feeling overwhelmed and panicked:

Limit a child's intake of news. For a child who is just learning about the small world around them, the concerns of the larger world can feel overwhelming, particularly when newspapers and news channels are designed to grab attention and stir up emotion. It's important to limit the amount of news your child watches or to ensure that they have access to their own gentler sources of news. There are news magazines for children which debate the issues in less emotive, steadier ways. Overall, however, news is best filtered and explained by parents.

Introduce slower, more hopeful understandings of the world. It's helpful if your child has the chance to discuss bigger issues with you. This doesn't means spending a lot of time in discussion, but it does mean explaining to him in simpler, less fear-based ways, how human beings can help with big issues such as discrimination, inequality or environmental concerns.

Emphasize the constructive meaningful process, rather than the large overwhelming issues. You might say something such as, *'We are trying hard to eat less meat as a family because it's a gentler way of living on this planet.'* Equally talk about others, including global figures, with a lower emotional tone. Be careful with derogatory comments; rather look for what the people who voted for that leader might be struggling with and how others are trying to take action.

Helping a Child to Slow Down

The complexity of the world makes itself known to a child not just through world issues such as the environment and inequality, but also imposes itself through the speed and intensity of ideas and demands. Whilst your child is young, your job is to help him move back into a gentler, protected space where he doesn't need to respond or do, or worry or think about things. Where he can recuperate and let go. You can do this by:

Routines and predictability. The busy, hectic, demanding nature of the world can take its toll on human beings. There seems no end to the amount we expect of ourselves. We become burnt out and lost, and it's harder to re-establish our own sense of balance.

Establishing predictable routines with your child helps him experience a balance between activity and rest. I talk to my children about having more active mornings and gentler afternoons. Things get a bit busier in the early evening, I say, and then quieten down for bed. Of course, this sometimes falls apart (especially at busier times of the year), but it's something they have become used to and it settles and steadies them.

Slowing and simplifying play. Not only does this world teach us to work faster, achieve more and compete harder; it also teaches us to over consume. For a child this can be consuming information, toys, games, food, amusement.

A writer I met in my 20s told me that he tried to balance the amount he consumed with the amount he produced. Being able to balance what we produce with what we consume is a very hard ask. I fail on nearly all fronts. But I do bear it in mind for both myself and my children. In an ideal world balancing consumption with production would mean that a child made up more stories, rather than just reading, he would draw more, make more and explore more.

This process starts early:

- Let children play with toys that are more open and demand more imagination and creativity.
- When you tell your child stories invite them to come in with details and events, taking some of the weight and creativity of developing the story.
- If they want sweets and treats suggest making these rather than buying them off the shelf.

5 POINTS TO REMEMBER FROM STEP 1

(If you only remember these five things you will have done well!)

- **Taking a simple approach to EQ means aiming to ease and clarify emotions**. It means regulating big, fast emotions and slowly supporting a child as he thinks about the slower, quieter emotions.
- **Your child's EQ is strengthened when he is allowed to develop his own pace and curiosity around emotions**. He becomes more comfortable and connected to his own responses. His language stretches and develops as he puts words to his emotional experiences.
- **These slow, careful understandings are particularly important in a society where we often create a sense of complexity around a child's emotions**. Complications arise because we attempt to:
  - Impose our own understandings onto our child's emotions, trying to shape and fix them
  - Use complicated labels and diagnostic terms
  - Seek to distract and save a child from mild emotional discomfort
- **This complexity can end up distancing a child from his own experiences**. He is unable to respond to or regulate his emotions. He feels confused and overwhelmed.
- Instead of analysing, diagnosing or distracting him from his emotions, **when you help your child learn to *slow down* and steady his emotions he begins to think through what they mean to him**. His emotions bring him closer to others and allow him to settle and tune in to his surroundings. He slowly develops his own emotional ease and expertise.

8

STEP 2:
ENCOURAGE ACCEPTANCE

Step 2 looks at encouraging acceptance. Acceptance of emotions is an important part of EQ. When you accept your child's emotions, rather than pushing away or stigmatizing her emotional responses, you begin to see her as a whole person. Her emotions are expressed more fully – and they bring a depth, warmth and energy to her experiences. She comes to understand her own preferences and values and she is better able to understand and regulate strong, difficult emotions.

Jack Kornfield, a Buddhist teacher and writer, tells a story of a small girl in a restaurant with her parents. A waitress comes over and the mother and father start ordering when the little girl interrupts, 'And I'd like a hotdog with fries and a cola,' she says quickly.

'No, no,' corrects her father, looking directly at the waitress. 'She'll have the meatloaf with mashed potato and a glass of milk.'

The waitress looks at the father and then smiles down at the little girl. 'What would you like on that hotdog, honey?' she asks.

'Ketchup,' the little girls says in a quiet voice.

When the waitress goes, the little girl turns to her parents. 'She thinks I'm real,' she says, her voice full of wonder, her eyes shining.

Being 'seen' is incredibly important to children. Although this example seems quite old-fashioned in today's world where children frequently order their own food, it nonetheless holds true. Children's experiences, thoughts and emotions can often be overlooked or side-lined.

It's easy to see how this happens. Our relationship with our child gets framed around the job of parenting. Decisions have to be made around her care and education; emotions and behaviours require management. A child needs to be fed and washed and changed, her thoughts and ideas shaped and channelled and corrected.

But what if, rather than 'parenting' our child we could enter into a *relationship* with her. What if she became someone with whom we were beginning a valuable new lifelong connection? Someone who we connect to with deep interest and curiosity; who we could enjoy and share ideas and experiences with; who was also, wonderfully enough, someone also interested in a relationship with us?

The word 'acceptance' comes from the Latin root 'to receive', as if to receive a gift.

It is easy to receive your child's love, sweet utterances and playful excitement when she is involved, colouring in, building something in her room, chatting easily about the trip with Daddy, holding your hand as she comes home from school. At these times you experience a sense of ease and order. But other times, emotions and behaviours can feel difficult and tense. Her worry about going to sleep, her negativity around new foods, her whiny, irritable voice. These are harder. Your instinctive reaction is to tighten up. You're not sure about having a deep relationship with a person who has these emotions!

At these times you emotionally distance yourself from her. You move into 'parenting mode', managing her moods and difficult behaviours. It seems she becomes 'difficult'. Perhaps you pull away sharply or maybe enter into a battle with the emotions to try and control them in some way or other.

STRUGGLING WITH EMOTIONS

During the times that you struggle and switch to parenting mode, your child doesn't like some of the emotions she feels either. She quickly picks up on the negative shift in you (for she knows your emotions and reactions all too well). Her emotions become more difficult. She starts to feel cut off and ashamed or hurt; things feel out of control, maybe angry, maybe panicky, but definitely bad. At these times your child may have the capacity to try and hold things back in the moment, pausing for a short while, but her emotions and thoughts and reactions have not stopped. Instead they stay very near the surface, hovering and taking up all of her attention and energy. When her emotions are unable to move on, they are constantly retriggered and the situation becomes more difficult.

Slowly, both sides get more stuck. It feels like you and your child are in an endless battle.

We know that struggling with emotions can intensify problems. In the old black-and-white films the guy gets stuck in quicksand. When he realizes with horror that he's sinking, he begins struggling, but the more he struggles the quicker the sand sucks him under. The same principle applies to struggles with our child's moods and behaviours.

It could be that the emotion that shows up most often for your child is anxiety. You see her anxiety rising and you start to struggle. You think: *'Oh no, I can't bear this. What's wrong with her? Why can't she just be like other children?'* Or it could be that you become frustrated about your own frustration: *'I should be able to cope with this. What am I doing to her?'* This struggle drains your energy and morale. It increases the intensity of your emotional response.

Kim John Payne, a child psychotherapist and writer, describes recurring struggle interactions as 'Repetitive Emotional Strain Injuries'. These tight, difficult interactions repeat and with each repetition we become more absorbed and fused with the difficult thoughts, feelings and behaviours. We struggle to manage them/change them/push them away.

In these interactions there is no space to consider a different way of responding. The thoughts insist that you should put your foot down. The focus becomes on stopping emotions and behaviours: '*Stop arguing, stop whining, stop being irritating, stop being negative,*' we say. Our child hears: '*Go away, this is too difficult for me. I don't like this part of you.*'

WHEN WE HOPE UPSETTING EMOTIONS WILL JUST GO AWAY

Parents deal with these tricky emotional struggles against a backdrop where the emotional life of families can be romanticized and smoothed over. We have a picture of how it would be if we were ideal parents, creating safe, secure, stable homes with the ideal children who are happy and contented.

Sometimes in an effort to live up to this idea, we try hard to cover over the cracks, particularly when we feel overwhelmed or panicky. We insist that our life is happier and more stable and that the emotions we all feel are warmer and more serene than in reality. Unfortunately trying to hold on to these types of ideas can become complicated, exhausting and confusing.

Some years ago I saw a couple who came to see me to discuss their son, Aran. The couple had separated but they had decided not to discuss this openly with Aran. 'Aran is so loved,' the father told me. 'We don't want him to feel upset, or responsible for the separation when nothing will really change for him. I have always travelled with work, so he is used to me not being around through the week and I am staying at the house most weekends. We have just told him that Mummy and Daddy are sleeping in different rooms because we have different routines.'

The difficulty was that the son seemed to know about the separation anyway. His mother described how Aran had begun complaining of anxiety at night time and constantly asked when his dad would be home. Aran was also becoming angrier and more aggressive during the day. His anger flared up over little things, such as taking a shower or helping to put the plates in the dishwasher.

There was his mother's concern that Aran had become secretive. She had discovered a book under Aran's mattress about divorce. 'He has always been a very open boy,' the mother told me. 'I think he stole this very grown-up book from the local library. I don't like what's happening to him.'

Aran's mother and father were struggling with the separation. Finding the process distressing themselves, the thought that Aran might also feel this way was unbearable and so they were attempting to shield him. When the book was discovered, rather than being seen as Aran's brave and clever way of understanding and making sense of things, his parents tied themselves (and him) up in further knots. The focus was on the more bearable issue of Aran having stolen a book.

Unlike the romanticized view, families can experience many upheavals and difficulties and our children respond emotionally to these difficulties. They experience sadness and vulnerability, distress and loss. We want to shield them from these feelings, but in our efforts to make these go away we restrict our child's ability to connect with us, to receive our support and to process these emotions.

Luckily, Aran wasn't going to give up. He was determined to understand and learn about the situation. He was fierce and resourceful. After discussing the situation with his parents they agreed that the most important thing would be for Aran to come into the sessions with me so that he could learn about the situation directly from his trusted adults.

Aran was quite an exceptional boy. When he saw that his parents were ready to talk to him about their separation, he leapt at the chance to talk. He told them that at first he couldn't understand what had happened, why his mum and dad didn't talk to each other and why his dad didn't live with them when he wasn't working. When he saw the book at the library he wanted to read it desperately, but he felt confused when his mum and dad denied that they were separating. 'I kept thinking that maybe you didn't love me anymore,' he said to his dad. 'I thought maybe you wanted to be away from us because I was asking you too many questions or maybe I was too boring because I don't play football or do cool things.' He continued looking at me: 'And then when my mum became angry at me for the book and for not sleeping, I thought, maybe Mummy wants to leave me as well.'

THE PROBLEM WITH SEEKING 'HARMONY'

When we think of Aran's situation, the idea that his parents needed to accept the situation and the emotions he was going through can be very appealing. We imagine stepping out of the struggle, listening to the emotions, working things through. We envisage developing a very harmonious, agreeable, fluid relationship with our child. We picture our child's emotions relaxing, we see her becoming happier, more open and more contented. But the reality of acceptance can be quite different.

When I was in my 30s, I went on a meditation retreat in Italy. We were up in the Umbrian mountains. The food was fantastic, the talks were open and illuminating. Things could not have been more blissful, but for my endlessly niggling back.

My supervisor for the week was a beautiful, olive skinned, calm guy. He sat on the floor in a position of simplicity and ease. He oozed calm. After a few days of trying to deal with my back, I moaned to him about the pain whilst I shifted and edged around the floor. It was driving me mad, I told him. I couldn't sit, couldn't concentrate, couldn't sleep.

He nodded encouragingly. 'Hmmm, hmmm,' he said, gazing at me with his big, brown eyes. 'I know, so painful,' he hummed.

'Yes,' I continued, 'and it's driving me bloody mad and I wish you had some more of those raised kneeling stools so I could just sit more comfortably.'

'Hmmm, yes,' he purred. 'It's hard to accept all these feelings and the emotions they bring.'

'He doesn't seem to be finding it hard to accept my feelings,' I thought.

His approach was much the same to many of the thoughts and experiences I had and shared with him. Sometimes my dramatics would tease a bigger smile, but mostly he observed my moods, thoughts and emotions pass like little fluffy clouds.

Having experienced this 'acceptance', I was left with the impression that 'accepting' meant feeling somewhat detached. It felt as though the aim was to relate to my emotions in a harmonious, removed way. I had to admit, this made some sense. After all, strong emotions could be annoying and painful and provoking. Fear can be strong, anger… strong, despair… strong. Why wouldn't he want to respond calmly to the emotions I was bringing, simplify them, concentrating instead on peaceful states?

Except that his peaceful state didn't seem to connect with my reality. Rather than feeling these calm emotions, I felt embarrassed at my whininess, my need for validation, my failure to achieve harmony. In those supervisions I felt itchy and agitated.

I'm not alone with experiencing some versions of acceptance as disconnected.

When her family cat died, one little girl told me how her very calm, laid-back uncle had responded with, 'We live, we die, that's the way of the world.'

'I didn't like him saying that. It felt like he didn't care,' she concluded.

Relating to your child from a place of acceptance isn't about controlling the amount of emotion being felt, smoothing things over, creating a manufactured harmony. It isn't simple agreement. It is more open, engaged, responsive and active.

ACCEPTANCE ISN'T ABOUT PLACATING
Sometimes, out of basic fatigue, I will move through the difficulties my children are having with each other, with themselves, with me, with a passive, '*I know, I know you want to watch X rather than Y*', '*Yes, you're annoyed because he keeps sticking his tongue out at you,*' as I usher them to bed/school/

the dinner table. This is better than becoming agitated and mad. But it will only work temporarily if their upset is not too big. Importantly, it is not acceptance.

When a child is experiencing big emotions, looking too quickly for harmony leaves her feeling disconnected, as though you have floated off somewhere. Somewhere non-attached.

Acceptance is more engaged. When a child experiences emotions, these emotions are delivering messages. Although we refer to 'struggling with emotions' as problematic, the real problem is pushing them away.

If the struggles we go through are through efforts to understand the meaning behind emotions then these struggles are important. Accepting your child's emotions doesn't mean feeling as provoked or uncomfortable as your child. But neither does it mean sitting with it whilst glazing over and being calm. Acceptance means being open to and listening to the emotions your child feels, giving them thought and attention, trying to understand them.

WHAT ENCOURAGING ACCEPTANCE LOOKS LIKE

So far I've talked a lot about what acceptance isn't and not very much about what it is.

When we think about encouraging acceptance around emotions it's important to reflect on how emotions behave. With an understanding of the nature of emotions, we can look at how acceptance allows you to help your child ground and steady herself in relation to these emotions.

EMOTIONS AS VISITORS WITH A MESSAGE

Your child experiences feelings, thoughts, judgements and memories that are many and various. Although her emotions can feel difficult, tiring, painful even, they have a purpose. They give her life value and direction, they help her communicate, problem solve and respond creatively and dynamically.

When I explain this to children, I often describe emotions as visitors.

I start by asking a child to tell me what their favourite emotions are. They typically say something such as, *'Excitement, like when it's going to be my birthday!'* Or *'Love, like when I see my mum and I get a cuddle.'* Or *'Fun emotions like I get when I'm laughing and playing.'*

I then ask them to tell me what the worst emotions they experience are. They might say: *'So angry I could tear everyone's heads off!'* Or *'Feeling really alone and frightened and far away from everyone.'* Or *'Feeling embarrassed and like everyone's going to find out.'*

Having invited them to think a bit I say:

'Let's imagine that your body is a house and that this house has lots of "emotion" visitors. You might have "Fun" visiting, or "Excitement" or "Love", and you open the door wide. Great, you think, I LOVE these emotions. You show them all around, your heart feels open, you feel happy.

'Now, sometimes your worst emotions arrive. Although you've locked the gate, and put a No Entry sign up, they seem to just arrive anyway. These emotions are stinky (I get the child to describe what fear, anger, humiliation look like – for example, smelly, disgusting with flies coming off them, rotten, squelchy). And when they're around, you notice your heart feeling heavy and closed. You don't want them to be around. This is going to ruin everything, you think.

'So, let's picture your favourite adult coming into your house. He/she doesn't seem to be surprised that there are good visitors and difficult visitors. In fact, your favourite adult seems to have time for both. When the Fun emotion

comes along, your favourite adult smiles and laughs with Fun. When Anger or Fear or one of the difficult emotions come along, your adult is somehow also okay. Your adult makes time for Anger/Fear when they say, "Tell me all about it, tell me what's wrong." He/she is patient and kind and listens. Then Anger /Fear seems less scary. They calm down.

'Now, the secret is that all of these emotions have a message. Something they need to tell us. Fun might be telling you: "You're ready to have a great time and use up loads of energy," or Loneliness may be saying: "You need a cuddle and a kiss and some good words whispered in your ear." Fear could whisper something like: "I think there might be something wrong but I'm not sure. I need an adult to help." And Shame may tell you, "I need to check a secret thing out with someone trusted."

'An emotion's job is to communicate something, but importantly, you need to know that it doesn't have words so it can be hard to be sure. Our job is to try and work out, often with our mum and dad, what helps the emotion relax and move on. That's the sign that it's delivered its message.'

Although this story is often told to children, we adults need to hear it as well. We need to know that we will experience many different emotions – sometimes they bring useful messages; sometimes they are just slightly unsettled. Importantly, we can allow all of them in. Emotions that we like will arrive but we'll also experience emotions that don't feel particularly comfortable. We don't get to choose who comes, but we can feel safe and okay around them.

THE BIG BLUE SKY AND THE WEATHER
The other story I tell is also about emotions: your child's difficult, overwhelming emotions. In this story her emotions are clouds

and she is the blue sky. This story helps your child ground herself and gain some perspective on her emotions. It creates a sense of space and reflection:

Imagine that the difficult emotions that your child experiences are stormy, heavy, grey clouds (weather). When your child isn't able to express her emotions, when she feels isolated and alone with them, these grey clouds seem thundery and large. She becomes overwhelmed by these storm clouds. She tries to push them away but they surround her. There is no room, no perspective.

With you by her side, this situation shifts and changes. You act as a clear mirror to the situation. Through you she notices that she can pan back from the emotional storm clouds (like a camera in a nature documentary) and gain a wider perspective. She gains a sense of capacity and space. She is the spacious blue sky through which storm clouds move.

From this perspective (again, through you), she sees her emotions as moveable, dynamic weather fronts; with this sense of calm perspective, she can think about these emotions. She stops being immersed in and struggling with her emotions; rather she feels calmer and more open. Together you experience the storm without feeling overwhelmed or fearful. You both reflect on the emotions without panic.

I find this sky and clouds metaphor very helpful. Rather than seeing your child and her emotions as one, she becomes someone experiencing sometimes difficult, sometimes overwhelming emotions and you become the person who helps her manage.

CREATING SPACE WITH ACCEPTANCE

The practice of standing with our child, mirroring openness to the emotions she experiences, without panic or struggle (being the big blue sky) allows her to fully share her feelings and difficulties. Acceptance creates the space for you get to know your child, to see her for who she is, to more fully allow her to express herself and be herself.

- When you practise responding with acceptance, you become more open to your child's feelings, thoughts and responses.
- You don't rush to make the more difficult emotions go away. You know that this is counterproductive. Rather, you recognize that with your support, her emotions will begin to shift in their own time.
- You learn to respond with an internal 'yes'. This yes lightens your load; it unhooks you from a sense of burden.
- Acceptance allows you to be less fearful; you feel less need to control your child and her experiences.
- And something new arrives. Rather than being stuck in repetitive struggles, your child's emotions help create a feeling of togetherness. They begin to make sense.

Responding with acceptance doesn't mean that we suddenly feel okay with the difficult interaction or emotions. That's not how it works. Rather, we give ourselves more space to think and respond, we notice tight restrictive beliefs and we stand back.

To return to the metaphor of sky and clouds, we see the difficult, angry, agitated emotions our child experiences as the storm clouds. We feel them, hear them and know them. But we also step back to hold a wider awareness, one where we are safe, our child is safe, there is no emergency,

ALLOWING VULNERABLE EMOTIONS TO EXPRESS THEMSELVES

You might remember the distinction between a child's more vulnerable, open, initial emotion and the 'secondary' defensive emotion described in chapter 2. Initial emotions are more vulnerable, open and expressive whilst secondary emotions tend to be defensive, tight and closed.

When we push emotions away, they come back as tense, defensive emotions. In easing and opening up your responses to emotions, your child is more able to experience the open, primary emotions which allow her to connect and relate to you.

A child who experiences her emotions as acceptable and knowable learns:

- Her feelings and thoughts are important to you
- She is seen by you; she is a whole person
- She is cared about
- Her understandings and perspectives are meaningful
- You enjoy learning about her

Carl Jung, the famous analyst, describes human growth as 'unfolding into wholeness'. When human beings push away or deny feelings and experiences, we make ourselves weaker. Our most vulnerable feelings and experiences allow us to let go of shame, to connect, to feel belonging and to understand.

ACCEPTANCE ISN'T...	ACCEPTANCE IS...
Disconnection	Opening up and understanding more
Endurance	Allowing change and movement
Agreement	Opening up difference and newness
Smoothing over	Feeling many emotions including those that are intense and difficult
Being disinterested	Curious and full of wonder
Avoiding	Staying with emotions, listening and trying to be with them

WHY ACCEPTANCE IS GOOD FOR EQ

ACCEPTANCE ENCOURAGES FEELINGS OF SAFETY

A child who experiences support and acceptance around her emotions learns to feel safe and secure. She doesn't have to push away feelings or force them out angrily. She knows they won't be dismissed or rejected and so she becomes comfortable and confident around them.

ACCEPTANCE ALLOWS COMFORTABLE EXPRESSION OF EMOTIONS

Through your acceptance, your child learns that her emotions are acceptable and that they make sense. This means she has more ability to notice and reflect on them. She feels comfortable expressing vulnerable emotions without moving quickly to either cover these up through fear or shame, or force them through in a more tense, angry way.

Since her emotions open up connection and help her to make sense of things, she enjoys testing out different ways of expressing them. When she cares about something she becomes animated and swift in her expression. If she wants to protect herself she might be fierce, indignant and righteous; or if the situation is calmer and softer she could take a more sorrowful and vulnerable approach. When she's pleased with herself she might try out feeling smug, or excited or relaxed. In essence, she becomes agile, expressive and responsive.

YOUR CHILD BECOMES MORE CONFIDENT IN RELATIONSHIPS

A child's emotions are such an integral part of her experience, that when they are accepted by the adults around her, she experiences herself as acceptable. And when she feels acceptable, she reaches out to others more, she communicates more and is more spontaneous and intimate.

Child psychologists talk about a child's ability to empathize with others and how important this is for her social development. A child who has experienced a range of emotions and has been able to make some sense of these is more able to empathize and understand others. She doesn't become unnerved by another child's tears and upset, she takes time to listen and understand. When her friend is upset, she thinks about her part in this but she also opens it up. I think of a child I saw recently sitting near her crying friend, and asked, 'Are you missing your mummy? Shall I give you a hug?'

YOUR CHILD CAN TUNE INTO EMOTIONS, BECOMING MORE RESPONSIVE AND EXPRESSIVE

Of course all of these abilities develop slowly over time with lots of shifts and changes, developments and setbacks. But if we accept that to be human is to feel a lot of emotions then we know that although emotions can feel like obstacles and hinderances, they are much, much more. Through having her emotional world accepted and responded to, your child learns directly that emotions allow connection and relatedness; that they are the way we understand, learn about and connect to the world.

A child who can tune in to her emotions, who learns to be comfortable with these, has a very solid base of emotional intelligence. This isn't to say that having a child who is more comfortable expressing her emotions will be a smooth ride. Being accepting often means *more* emotions to think about and respond to. When we are open to accepting emotions, we also have to be open to shifting, changing and accommodating in response to them.

HOW TO RESPOND WITH ACCEPTANCE: KEY SKILLS

'Between stimulus and response, there is a space, and in that space is our power to choose, and it's in that choice that lies our growth and freedom.'
Victor Frankl, psychiatrist and writer

'We have more possibilities available in each moment than we realize.'
Thich Nhat Hanh, Buddhist monk

PAUSE AND STEP OUT OF THE STRUGGLE

Responding to a child's anxiety, avoidance and frequent behavioural difficulties can be a minefield. Difficult emotions exert a strong pull on children, but also on parents. Their force is quickly felt by all involved. In other words, they are contagious.

When your child feels anxious, angry, determined or controlling, you begin to feel similarly emotionally charged. And if you look like you're unaffected or feeling just too relaxed (think back to my super-chilled meditation supervisor), then your child will increase the pressure.

Accepting your child's emotions is not a passive process. To accept an emotion you need to know what it is and what it might be communicating. This means slowing down/pausing.

In responding with acceptance, the most important part is to pause. Here's how it might look:

- When you pause, your intention is to slow down habitual responses and patterns and allow space.
- When you pause, you might notice yourself thinking, *'Her behaviour is way out of control, I am going to put my foot*

down.' Or *'I will show her that no means no.'* Or you might simply be thinking, *'I don't know what to do, I can't help her.'*

- These thoughts can be very emotional and can either 'fuse' us into battle with our child or shut us down. By 'fuse', I mean plug us right in so that our emotions and thoughts become immovably stuck to the situation. We identify with these emotions and thoughts as facts: *'This is what I think about my child's emotions – it is the only possible way to see this situation.'*

- Part of de-fusing these thoughts is simply to notice them: *'Oh there's that thought again.'* Labelling it as a thought makes it easier to unhook from it. Some therapists write the thought down on a piece of paper and place it to the side of your visual frame. It is there but it is not dominating your attention.

- Being less preoccupied with habitual thoughts means you have greater mental space and feel less agitated. Your breathing slows down and you're more able to speak slowly, kindly and comfortably. In response, your child starts to feel open and comfortable herself.

If your child is distraught and upset, the most important thing is that she knows you're present and with her. It can take a while for her to be able to speak, so showing you're not in a rush is helpful. You can crouch down and move nearer; she might want to sit on your lap or close to you or perhaps she wants a bit of space. Some physical connection helps orientate her to you so you can put a hand on her arm if she is able to tolerate that.

BE CURIOUS ABOUT THE EMOTION

If your child is feeling a lot of heated emotions, she will likely have difficulty putting her feelings into words, but as she gets older (over six or seven years) she might be able to explain more.

Your role is to gently open up a space for her. You might start with: *'Oh darling, I can see that so much is going on for you.'*

Wait a little bit. After a pause you could say, *'Can you tell me a little bit about it?'*

Overall, you're aiming to talk less and listen more, but she will probably need prompts to know that you are listening and connecting with her. Here are some easy prompts:

- *'So what you're saying is...'*
- *'That makes sense to me.'*
- *'Mmm...'*
- *'If feels as though...'*
- *'So tell me if I'm understanding this properly. On the one hand ... And on the other hand...'*
- *'That sounds like...'*
- *'Yes, I see...'*
- *'I imagine you might feel...'*
- *'Uh-huh.'*
- *'Am I getting this right?'*

Remember to keep any suggestions very simple – stay away from complexity. You might use feeling words such as worried, sad, upset, cross, relieved, mixed-up.

When you pause and notice your own instinctive reactions to your child's emotions without pulling away or trying to block her responses, you allow yourself to become curious. Your child can slow down. She doesn't have to force her emotions out defensively. She is more likely to express simpler, more open emotions.

When your child can let you know how she feels (be it anger, sadness, jealousy, panic, fear) without worrying that you will react negatively, then these emotions become linked to safety, openness and connection. We saw this in chapter 3 when we spoke about acknowledging and being open to all a child's emotions, even the defensive ones that seem to push you away. When her emotions are openly received, her sense of struggle and fear begin to fade. Although she might start out expressing emotions that are ambiguous or defensive, the calm and the connection help her express the quieter, more hidden emotions.

I'll be honest with you: this is not always easy to do! A child who is jerky and erratic in maintaining a connection will need a lot of gentleness, humour and flexibility from an adult. Your child needs *you* to be the one to pause, find an opening and respond to her efforts. Her behaviours or arguments might trigger your frustration or annoyance and so finding a way to connect with her emotions, but also allowing things to settle, takes time and effort and the capacity to forgive yourself when it goes wrong!

PEEL BACK OVERUSED EMOTIONAL LABELS

Sometimes emotions exist in an unnamed whirlwind of feelings. At other times they seem quickly recognizable, arriving with their own ready-made label. Ready-made labels can be rather difficult in that they can link the emotion to a particular situation or person. Your child might feel upset and attach that emotion to going out: '*I hate going out,*' or to a person: '*Oli is so irritating.*'

These emotions can get hidden by their label. For example, your child might tell you that she is bored: '*I'm bored with being at home*', '*I'm bored with this food*', '*I'm bored with school.*' Taking the label at face value, you try to think of other places to go, different foods to try, ways to make school interesting but it doesn't seem to affect the bored feeling.

Listening to and accepting emotions doesn't mean *agreeing* with how your child interprets them. Acceptance means acknowledging and making space for the emotion. When you feel an emotion has been labelled too quickly it's helpful to slow things down and step back so you can both give the emotion some more thought.

Giving the emotion your full attention means:

- Standing apart from the emotion (remember being the blue sky noticing the grey clouds)
- Soothing and comforting her
- Trying to connect with what the emotion feels like/what might have triggered it
- Helping your child notice what helps/what doesn't

How to Peel Back a Label

Let me give an example of how you might work with 'bored'. If a child feels *bored* then she needs entertaining. But what if her boredom is more like, *'I can't relax'*, *'I don't know how to play anymore'*, *'I feel a bit worried/disappointed/sad'*, *'I feel alone'*?

Here's what you might do when a child says, *'I'm bored'*:

- **Separate the child from the emotion**. *'So there's a "bored" feeling upsetting you...'* Or you might simply use *'you feel'* to create space between child and emotion: *'So you're feeling a bit of boredom,'* rather than *'So you're bored.'*
- **Find out more about the emotion**. Maybe start with, *'Does "bored" feel heavy?'*, *'Has it got a bit of "I can't feel like anything is good here" in it?'*, *'When did you feel it come?'*, *'Has the feeling just arrived or has it been around for a bit?'*
- **Look for ways to connect that help a child soften and open up the feeling**. *'When you're sitting on my lap now having a cuddle, do the bored feelings seem to reduce, move away or change in any way?'*
- **Acknowledge additional feelings**. *'Has bored got any other feelings that have come along with it that we should pay attention to?'* (Perhaps tiredness, sadness, loneliness, need for connection.)

- **End with an invitation to stay connected for a while**. *'Would you like to stay here with me for a bit? Will you sit here in the chair near me whilst I finish this job? We can chat and see if the feelings feel more settled.'*

Quite often a child will struggle to answer your questions, but you'll notice that the feeling shifts. Your child relaxes. She feels calm and reflective. Of course, your child might say, *'I need a new game to play, I want you to make a playdate with X.'* Consider these types of suggestion lightly. You might say, *'Mmm. They're interesting suggestions. But stay with me and have a cuddle for a bit.'* Most often *'bored'* or other common emotions need time and kindness rather than extra games or lots of activity.

WHEN A DIFFICULT EMOTION GETS LINKED TO A PERSON OR THING

When a child attaches an emotion to a person, thing or event, it's worth thinking about how much of the emotion is about the problematic *'thing'* and how much is your child's need for connection and help with the emotion.

Say, for example, your child tells you that she feels really upset because her brother keeps looking at her. It's helpful to balance out a focus on her brother's behaviour (it may actually be annoying) with a focus on the emotion and your child's wider needs.

You can start by acknowledging that she feels annoyed about her brother. That it can feel very annoying to ask someone to stop doing something but they don't. But pause on the feeling, not the brother.

Now if you feel her brother's behaviour has overstepped the line then this can be dealt with; but take the time before this to help your daughter to reflect on how she feels and what she needs. She might need you to go downstairs and dig out her art materials so she can settle and have some quiet time. She could need to be near you for a bit, reading whilst you sort things out. Her brother might be the least of her worries.

ACCEPT THE EMOTION BUT NOT THE BEHAVIOUR

Accepting and opening out emotions and thoughts *doesn't* mean accepting behaviours that are aggressive or damaging.

For example, a child might be frustrated at a new toy that is difficult to put together. If she goes to push the toy off the table or break it in some way, putting a clear limit on that behaviour (*'We can't let the game get broken, let's put it down and sit together on the sofa'*) helps focus on the underlying emotions.

By being clear and direct and moving her away from easy, defensive, controlling reactions, you help create space for her quieter, vulnerable, open emotions.

5 POINTS TO REMEMBER FROM STEP 2

- **When you nurture your child's emotional intelligence, you steady and accept *all of* her emotions**. Rather than deciding on the emotions that she should/shouldn't have, you make space for *all* emotions – be they tight and frightened, giddy and silly, or sad and unsettling.
- **Accepting a child's emotions means stepping back from taking action or trying to shift her emotions**. Instead, you slow down and listen with curiosity and kindness.
- **Acceptance may bring a paradox**. When emotions are pushed away, they tend to become intense and difficult to shift; but when they are accepted, they change and adapt and develop.
- **Accepting a child's emotions means**:
  o Supporting her through experiencing the emotion
  o Being a secure, steady presence so that she feels safe
  o Slowing down and steadying your reaction so she can do the same
  o Helping her to make sense of the emotion
  o Showing her that emotions come and go, that whatever emotions she experiences, you love and accept her
- **Acceptance doesn't mean smoothing emotions over** and hoping they will pass. It doesn't mean allowing behaviours that are hurtful or damaging. And it doesn't mean agreeing. Instead, it means giving your child the support to express and reflect on how she feels.

9

STEP 3:
RESPOND WITH COMPASSION

*'We need to take a less narrow look at our child's problems
and, instead, see them as windows of opportunity, a way
of exploring and understanding all facets of our child's
development. If we can understand the underlying
developmental process, we can see a child's struggles
as signs of striving toward growth – instead of chronic
problems or attempts to aggravate adults.'*
Dr Stanley Greenspan, child psychiatrist

*Whilst EQ develops through opening out and leaning-in
to emotions, for a child some emotions can seem stuck and
anxious. In an effort to deal with these emotions, some children
try to avoid not only thinking about them, but also the situations
which seem to trigger them. In this step we'll think about how
you can use a compassionate approach when your child gets
stuck in cycles of avoidance. When you respond to difficult
emotions with compassion you help your child through fear
and avoidance, enabling him to connect with more resourceful,
curious, adaptive emotions.*

*I met Krish when he was nine years old. He sat on my
sofa with his arms tightly crossed and head down. 'I'm not
interested in talking to someone like you,' he told me. He*

stood firm on this, it was a definite 'no', so we agreed that his mum would 'do the talking' whilst he listened.

Krish's mum explained that he lived with her and his dad and his younger brother. Although Krish had always been more emotional than his brother, over the past year he seemed to be almost constantly irritated and annoyed by things. He was irritated at being woken up, annoyed that he had to go to school, cross when he was asked to help clear up, frustrated when it was time for bed. Previously he had enjoyed going to friends' houses but in the last few months he would say things such as, 'Aran winds me up, I can't be bothered to go to his house,' or 'Football's boring and anyway I'm no good at it.'

Recently there had been a school trip and Krish kept moving between wanting to go and not wanting to go. 'He got really upset about it in the evenings, telling me he was going, but then the next day he would be adamant that there was no way he was going at all, telling me that I was pressurizing him,' explained his mum.

Krish's mum was thoughtful in how she described his difficulties. She tried to stroke his head in the session, but he pulled away. She told me that Krish frequently got angry with her and would shout, 'Leave me alone, you're the worst mum I could have!' before going off to his room and slamming the door.

'I can't catch up with his emotions,' she reflected. 'I sympathize. He gets upset and sometimes opens up a little, but then, just as quickly, he gets angry and tells me to go away. I suggest things that might help and he gets defensive. We seem to repeat the same stuck, snappy interactions over and over.'

Krish's mum was trying hard to be open to his emotions, accepting of his feelings and empathic, but she was worried and concerned. She recognized that Krish's stuck emotions were stopping him from doing things that had been very important to him but they also seemed to be getting in the way of his relationships with family and friends.

WHEN EMOTIONS AND BEHAVIOURS GET STUCK

In Step 2, Acceptance, I described emotions as visiting, passing on a message and then leaving. The idea is that the more parents can model acceptance of emotions for a child, the more the child can experience these emotions as potentially meaningful and harmless. Without fear or panic, he has a greater ability to take on board their message before letting them pass.

Whilst acceptance is a very important tool, life is complicated. The various demands and changes in a child's life can mean that his emotions aren't always steadied and made sense of in the here-and-now. If the discomfort around particular emotions feels intense, a child not only pushes the emotions away, but also the situation he perceives to be triggering it.

Let me give you some examples of the ways in which a child might push away both the emotions and the situations linked to these:

- Your ten-year-old has a difficult time at a friend's house. He feels isolated and nervous and unsure what to do. The next time a visit is suggested, the feelings of nervousness and anxiety reappear. He instinctively decides that it would be better if he didn't go. He begins to feel fearful and defensive whenever further visits are suggested and wants to stay at home.
- You are driving with your daughter when another car drives into the back of your car. You are both shaken, but no one

is hurt and there is only some minor damage to the car. After this, your daughter wants to avoid going in the car. You decide not to push it, but two weeks later she is still refusing and if anything, is more adamant that she won't drive with you.

- Your seven-year-old gets very upset when you go out. He refuses to stay with his grandmother or the babysitter. His upset remains just below the surface whilst you're gone, escalating when he needs to eat, bath or get ready for bed.
- After a difficult match where she missed an important goal, your child starts pulling back from football. She doesn't want to go to practice, and she has stopped playing football with her friends at school.

Although in these situations you try to listen and help your child through, he wants to avoid both the emotions and the situation – and he pulls away.

Whilst some of these difficulties can be temporary and linked to specific situations, change is needed when these difficult emotions and behaviours begin to hang around for more than a week or two and impact significantly on important areas:

- Family relationships and interactions
- Access to joyful, relaxed friendships
- His capacity to learn, challenge himself and develop key skills (such as reading, writing, swimming, being independent)
- His ability to have fun and explore
- His independence and freedom

Before we go any further it's important to mention that these difficulties can happen with any child. This is a normal part of life (we looked at this in Part One when we talked about Good Enough Parenting and being in and out of sync with a child).

Your growing child will naturally make attempts to resolve emotions on his own without coming to you, since he spends much of the day at school and there will be many times when he is at friends' houses, playing sports, attending clubs when he needs to find a way to cope with big emotions. But when he tries to manage by pushing not just the emotions, but also the situations linked to these away, the original emotions can become very stuck and tight and difficult.

Just as with the process of reconnecting and repairing that we spoke about in relation to Good Enough Parenting, it's essential that you and he have a way of reconnecting emotionally to help him experience these emotions and work through the avoidance.

MOVING BEYOND ACCEPTANCE: RESPONDING WITH COMPASSION

As we saw in Step 2, when parents encourage acceptance toward emotions, their child becomes more comfortable pausing and noticing his emotions. He can put words to his experiences. The emotions, having passed on their message, relax and go.

Unfortunately, if a child begins to not only push the emotions away, but also the situations he links to those emotions, then the emotions become more stuck. Since the emotions are now caught up in avoidant behaviours, opening out and accepting the emotions – without being able to help shift things – becomes ineffective. The behaviour reminds him that the emotion is problematic and that he can't deal with it.

At a certain point you know that something has to change. This is where a compassionate approach comes in. Responding with compassion helps when a child's emotions are pushing him to avoid situations. Through compassionate change you seek to emotionally support your child and help him to move through difficult and stuck emotional responses.

There are two aspects to responding compassionately:

1. Slowly and kindly reconnecting with your child around the difficult emotions so that he feels steadier and safer, and is more open to influencing and changing stuck patterns.
2. Breaking down a stuck situation so that he can balance his emotions and move through avoidance.

A compassionate approach is warm and kind but also steady and confident. This combination of being warm and steady but also focused helps signal to a child's anxious emotions that he is safe and secure and that he has your support. You are seeking to connect with your child emotionally whilst also helping him reduce avoidance.

When you are acting compassionately, you actively think about how to work *through* not just the emotions but also the avoidant emotional behaviours with your child. You look for ways to *join with* your child so that you both have more direct influence over stuck emotions and problems with avoidance.

WHY RESPONDING WITH COMPASSION IS GOOD FOR EQ

We would all rather a child didn't struggle with feeling overwhelmed or anxious. When he's your child, watching him pull back, becoming miserable and frustrated, is upsetting and bewildering. You worry that he is distressed, but you also notice that he seems defeated and bothered.

And yet these emotional difficulties are part of being human. They present us with the opportunity to help our child open up capabilities and skills. When he has your compassion and support to move through emotional difficulties, he gains a deep understanding of relationships, collaboration, change and emotions.

Compassionate change is not in essence about end points or setting goals (although we do identify steps that we can take in trying to rebalance fearful emotions). Rather, it's about helping your child to be more expansive and curious and emotionally agile.

COMPASSION BRINGS EMOTIONAL AGILITY

Let me explain what I mean by being emotionally agile. When we talk about emotions we often think that we feel one emotion at a time. We see our friend, we feel happy. Then we get an e-mail telling us we are overdue with a payment; the happiness shifts out of the way and we feel burdened. Each emotion seems to come in as a response to a given trigger.

But what if emotions are far more interactive and busy? Rather than simply being pleasant or unpleasant responses to a situation, they are around both before and after the trigger, carrying ideas and skills that we might need. So we might be in a situation where a fear emotion is present. Its skill is to identify problems and help us take action or flee if need be. But there will also be other emotions present. Vulnerable emotions which help us find and get support from trusted friends. Brave emotions which know how we can move forward and work through fear and avoidance.

Dealing with all these differing emotions, knowing how to access the emotions we need and not becoming overwhelmed by just one emotional response, requires agility.

Through my work I see many children and families who have moved through emotionally stuck situations. When a child's parents support him compassionately to face difficult situations and problems, he learns about accessing different emotional responses. He discovers that although fear emotions seem dominant and he feels blocked and anxious, he has other emotions that feel more resourceful and encouraging. In other words, he becomes more agile in working with his emotions.

COMPASSION BRINGS CONFIDENCE

The process of being compassionately supported gives a child an expanded sense of what he is capable of. Having managed to move through his difficulties he is more willing to take risks, to fail, to be creative and resourceful. He learns to become comfortable with discomfort and understands how to break difficulties down into manageable chunks.

The combination of having the experience of change but also parental support through this means he can lean on strong, positive emotions. He learns to recognize the things of value in his life. Often children tell me they 'don't care' about friends, activities, schoolwork, but as they learn how to move through stuck emotions and behaviours, they get back their old sense of enjoyment and adventure around these things.

HOW TO RESPOND WITH COMPASSION: KEY SKILLS

WHAT COMPASSIONATE ENCOURAGEMENT CAN LOOK LIKE

RATHER THAN...	TRY...
Blaming	**Acknowledging**
'If you had practised rollerblading before with me then you wouldn't have got hurt.'	'This is your first time, it's hard at the beginning.'
Negatively comparing	**Making positive comparisons**
'Look at the little boy over there – he's not scared...'	'I remember finding this really tough when I started.'
Distracting	**Connecting**
'Oh look – there are lots of exciting floats over there...'	'I can see you're working so hard, you're figuring out just what you need to do.'

RATHER THAN...	TRY...
Minimizing/invalidating	**Validating**
'It's a really easy book, this should be simple.' 'There's nothing to be scared of.'	'There are a lot of worries to manage. I can see how much brave effort you're putting in.'
Pressurizing	**Slowing down**
'Come on, do it quickly, we need to go home!'	'You're doing really well. Let's take as much time as we need.'
Ending abruptly	**Ending with a soft positive**
'Right, let's finish now.'	'Do five more pedals with me holding you and then we can tell Daddy how well we've done.'

BE A COMPASSIONATE GUIDE

Trying to support your child through avoidance can be tiring and frustrating. Your child becomes very sensitive to pressure so you try to take things slowly but you worry that he is disconnecting from the things he used to care about. You desperately want to find a way to shift the situation. You want to help him to see through the emotional wall so that he and you can gain influence over these difficulties.

In order for your child to fully learn how to deal with anxiety and avoidance, he needs you to be his guide. This means finding an internal space from where you can attend to his emotions and understand his dilemmas, but nonetheless also calm and centre yourself so that you don't get overwhelmed. It means being patient and slow and steady.

This isn't easy. You try to take things slow, but he seems to switch off. You try and plead with him in order to 'wake him up' or motivate him. Or you might find yourself highlighting the negative consequences or comparing:

- *'You're falling behind in your reading; all the rest of the class will be reading books from the junior library and you'll still be on the little kids books.'*
- *'If you won't get into the car with me, we can't go to see Granny and she will get very sad and lonely.'*
- *'This behaviour is really silly. Your five-year-old cousin isn't worried about X.'*

Unfortunately this can be counterproductive. Instead of helping a child to feel more courageous and capable, these responses increase the difficult emotions your child feels – and he pulls back.

Your child needs to know that you are comfortable, clear-eyed and steady. You are his guide and he can find ways through this. As you reflect and then respond with thought and care, he learns to do this as well. So instead of highlighting the negatives, listen and connect to his emotions:

- *'I can see you're having a hard time with this.'*
- *'Can you tell me how it feels when you think about going into the car?'*
- *'Where can you feel it in your body?'*
- *'What goes through your mind?'*

Listening and trying to understand how the difficult emotions feel can seem like you are pulling your child backward, *into* the difficulty – almost encouraging it. The reality is that the more your child feels you recognize and understand these emotions, the more he opens up to your guidance and the quicker his confidence is to recover. Sometimes a child can answer these questions – at other times they push them away – that doesn't matter, you've set the tone for beginning to approach and sort through the avoidance.

YOUR JOB IS TO PROVIDE LOTS OF COMPASSION

When you respond in an openly compassionate way, your child is more likely to connect with braver, calmer feelings. Never worry about being too sugary or too emphatic in your reassurance. He'll soon tell you if you're over doing it but will rarely say, 'Please be more encouraging'! I find simple phrases such as, 'You're doing so well', 'You're such a brave boy', 'You're working so hard' in a warm, kind voice work best.

OVERCOMING ANXIETY AND AVOIDANCE WITH SIMPLE STEPS

When a child experiences anxious emotions and wants to avoid a situation, the only way for his confidence to return is for him to learn, through directly re-experiencing it, that the situation is not to be feared, that he can manage it, that he is okay, that he is safe.

Through responding with compassion, your attention is on helping your child feel secure and safe. This happens when you are aware and responsive to his feelings of fear and overwhelm whilst also being steady and kind and slowly nudging him forward.

When you act compassionately, you are aware that rushing him into the avoided situation too abruptly or aggressively can act to ramp up his fears again, leaving him panicking. He digs his heals in and the anxiety and avoidance become worse. Responding with compassion means that instead of rushing him through, you acknowledge his feelings and slowly help him think about how he can begin to feel more comfortable and at ease in a situation. One good way of helping your child to feel safer around change is to talk about creating steps on a ladder.

How to Explain the Stepladder

To make the stepladder more concrete I look for examples that a child can relate to. Pets are ideal for this as they often need help with anxious and avoidant behaviours and a child will understand why being kind, but steady is helpful.

Let me give you an example of the type of conversation I have with a child who has had an anxious puppy to help him understand how anxiety can get addressed in steps:

'So let me tell you how this works: You know how your puppy was really frightened of cars when she first came home? Your mum said she was even afraid when we walked past your car on the drive. She used to shake and then bark. Can you think back to how you got her used to being around cars?'

Hopefully a child will say something along the lines of, 'We helped her see that it wasn't so frightening by taking things slowly,' or something of the sort. I then continue: 'Well you made sure you cuddled her a lot and told her it was okay but took her near to a car that wasn't moving so she could sniff it and check it out. And then when she was used to that, you slowly opened a door and left it open so she could sniff around inside and you gave her lots of strokes. And then you carried her so she could see the cars on the road...'

If the child is still on board, I go on: 'Each of the things you did with the puppy was like a step on a ladder. When the puppy was comfortable with something, you took a further step.' You could then ask: 'Where do you think the steps on this ladder were taking her?' A child might come in with a funny or random answer. That's no problem. I just say, 'Each step on the ladder helped her to feel more and more brave around cars.'

When a child relates a problem to another person (or animal!), his brain is less anxious, and he can take the information in more easily. Moreover (particularly with a pet), he is often able to understand why the animal needs help and will see its fear and avoidance through a compassionate lens. This understanding provides a background of compassionate, connected understanding when you are helping him to overcome his own worry.

Working Out the Steps on the Ladder

In thinking about the situation your child avoids, you might work out a step either by thinking of:

- A small version of the feared situation
- Or (if the activity can't be broken down) doing the avoided thing, but for a short period of time.

If your child (like Krish at the beginning of this chapter) is avoiding a range of things, start with something small but concrete. Take care to choose something more manageable for the first try. For example, he might avoid schoolwork but this holds a lot of anxiety and seems big. He stands more chance of getting comfortable with something he avoids lightly, like trying out his new scooter.

The first step in moving through avoidance is the hardest. Luckily, if a task is bigger or more frightening, then there is almost no step too small (I'll talk next about working out the right level of engagement). When I'm chatting to a child about something he has been avoiding, we talk about helping his emotions not feel too uncomfortable by starting off with a *very teeny weeny* try. He could be anxious about eating vegetables and we'll agree that he only has to touch the green bean with his finger and then he's done. Now, if this will really be too easy for him then start off with something slightly harder, such as touching the green bean with his tongue or eating a teeny tiny, grain-of-rice-sized portion.

Make sure the steps are not too far apart in difficulty. If your child gets stuck between steps, you can comment that his emotions are having to work hard to adjust and feel safe. Explain that it's good to help them along a bit by making the next step less challenging. A child who has this kind, compassionate support, who feels his emotions steady, will notice his anxiety reducing. He'll feel safer and more confident.

Finding 'Just Right': Balancing Anxiety and Braveness

Helping your child get over avoidance works best when you are working through difficulties on the edge of his fear. This is the place where his fear is not too strong, not too weak. It's the place where your child feels the anxiety and desire to avoid, but he isn't overwhelmed or panicky so he can also connect to the desire to shift the fear. When you respond to his anxiety compassionately, you help him find this 'edge' by balancing kindness and support, with steady curiosity and a gentle persistence.

Let's take an example of a child that is scared of getting into water.

You identify the step on the ladder that feels okay for him, but having dipped a toe in, he might decide he has tried enough, and he pulls away. You know he could manage more. The effort to get to the swimming pool has been big. It feels like, despite all the planning, your child is not really trying.

So that you don't get stuck in these kinds of 'non-tries' it's helpful to prepare your child for this *beforehand.* When you take a compassionate approach you want to make sure a child has a kind, comfortable understanding of what happens emotionally when we work through difficulties. I find the following explanation helpful in preparing a child:

'Our emotions have a way of telling us when things are "just right". Like with Goldilocks when she was testing out the bears' porridge. She knew when the porridge was too hot, and when it was too cold and lumpy. She chose the "just right" porridge.

'Now, anxiety might shout out, "Too hot!" when you go anywhere near water, but you have other emotions around which are a bit calmer and steadier. They assess a situation. They know that staying away is "too cold". When we give the emotions a bit of time to explore a situation, they are able to feel where the "just right" spot is. This is where the anxiety isn't too high, but nor is it relaxing in a hammock, totally switched off.

'So, the "just right" spot with water isn't about keeping completely away, it's about finding the point where the anxiety isn't too big, or too small. Where you can feel the anxiety, but your brave emotions help you manage just a bit of it.'

Having explained this ahead of time, when you get to the pool, you then tell your child that, together, your job is to help his emotions work to find the 'just right' spot. The place where the brave emotions help to balance the worried emotions. Get your child to sit at the edge of the pool with you whilst you both variously try out different levels of getting into the water. Use your instinct to pick a safe starting position, for example you might get him to sit on the side with you, dangling his legs in.

Tell your child that you need feedback from both his anxious and brave emotions: 'When we sit here dangling our legs in, what is anxiety saying? What does braveness say?'

Responding compassionately is essential when there are setbacks. If your child is having difficulty feeling brave, then your compassionate presence can help. When you're warm, validating and open, interested in his suggestions and feedback (not frustrated), and when you are fully prepared to try things out as well, then he is more likely to relate to these emotions within himself.

With each step on the ladder, you help that connection to braveness. To do this you keep compassionately collaborating with your child and you keep involved. And once he has engaged with just a bit of braveness, then that ladder step is done.

Taking Things Slowly

Although I have spoken about finding the edge, the just right spot, between anxiety and braveness, it is always helpful to be patient. Avoidance comes from a sense that fearful, anxious emotions are unbearable. The more patient and collaborative you are at first, the quicker your child relaxes and builds up confidence. At the first attempt, you focus on ensuring that the task is broken down to its smallest, meaningful step. Your job then is to make sure your child accesses feelings of braveness and 'can-do' each time he approaches the anxious feelings.

If Progress Stalls, Don't be Afraid to Go Back a Few Rungs on the Ladder

Sometimes a child will do well on one occasion but when you go back to do some further practice, he digs his heels in. He feels anxious again, 'change' has lost its novelty. This is really common since anxiety builds up once we've gone away. Your job is to re-find 'just right' again. And if that means moving back down the ladder then so be it.

Say your child is worried about getting into the swimming pool. Yesterday he climbed in and even blew a bubble in the water but today he is refusing to get in. You want to make sure he stays engaged rather than completely pulling away, so let him move back a few steps. Don't worry about him returning to putting his face in the water again. The most important thing is that he is involved with the task so go back to letting him climb down the ladder again. Often, when we soften the demand, our child relaxes and begins to engage with moving through his fear once more.

Breaking down anxious avoidance into small steps can be used when a child avoids a specific situation, but also when he avoids a particular journey or social situation. The basics stay the same: you and your child work through ways of breaking down that situation into manageable steps and then you get going. As above, progress can feel like two steps forward and one back (or sometimes two back) but when your child has your care and patient collaboration, his courage increases and he can get over the difficulties.

BE COLLABORATIVE

In supporting your child compassionately through anxious emotions, your aim is to help him balance out fearful and anxious emotions rather than too directly or quickly trying to move through avoidance. Collaborating with a child takes time and effort but trying to *impose* change without being collaborative is almost always counterproductive. He feels overwhelmed and out of control, he's not able to consciously feel resourceful, he digs his heels in and struggles quickly intensify.

The more you collaborate kindly and openly with your child, the greater his ability to learn about emotions and the different ways he can be resourced by them. He learns that problems are attached not just to fear and anxiety but also to the emotions that can help them soften and shift. These 'determined' emotions include love, courage, enjoyment and curiosity.

Separating Children from their Problems

Unfortunately, the difficulty with trying to be collaborative is that at first your child is likely to react when you talk about something he is avoiding with a quick 'no'. The relief this powerful no provides for your child means he determinedly pulls back, and it can be hard to draw him out again. So, given the importance of collaboration, it's helpful to have a few different skills up your sleeve to help get your child on board.

One of the most important skills is to separate your child out from the problem. Psychologists refer to this as 'externalizing the problem', but this does the process an injustice. It is far more fun than it sounds.

One of the best examples of externalizing a problem is 'Sneaky Poo'. Sneaky Poo often gets used by psychologists working with chronically constipated children.

I'll give you an example from a conversation I had with a six-year-old boy called Gus.

Gus' dad told me that when he was about four years old, he heard him shriek in the toilet. He realized that Gus' poo had become hard and it had been very painful when he tried to go to the toilet. Naturally, from this time on Gus had been reluctant to poo. The doctor had prescribed a natural laxative which made his poo soft, but Gus seemed to remain worried and continued to avoid the toilet. The laxatives softened some of the poo but Gus was holding the rest in and the old poo became hard. Poor Gus, by the time he came to see me, like lots of children in his situation, he wasn't noticing signs that he needed to poo. Since he was regularly taking laxatives, he was also soiling himself. He felt ashamed and avoidant and his confidence was really low.

After listening to his dad for a bit, I turned to Gus: 'Gus, I think I need to tell you about Sneaky Poo and the daft tricks he plays on the kids I see.'

Gus looked uneasy.

I continued: 'Sneaky Poo is a real pain. Kids tell me that he gets them into trouble with their mum and dad, he can be really embarrassing and smelly in school and he makes everyone fed up!'

'I think he might be visiting us. What can we do about him?' said Gus's dad (who was good at playing along).

'Oh no, has he been causing you loads of problems too?' I said in mock surprise.

Gus laughed and hid his face behind his hands. 'He is my biggest enemy,' he said in a muffled voice.

'You and me both,' I replied. 'He really is a sneaky character. And because he is so sneaky, I'm going to tell you all about him.'

'Do other kids have him?' asked Gus.

'Oh yes, so many,' I assure him wholeheartedly.

I then told Gus all about Sneaky Poo, how he lives in Poo Land which is a very faraway place that he can get to down the toilet. How Sneaky Poo forgets where he's going and gets carried away hiding and playing tricks. Although he can be a pain, Sneaky Poo isn't a bad poo, he can be a bit silly, but with a little bit of help from us he begins remembering where he needs to go.

I asked Gus if he would be interested in being Sneaky Poo's coach.

'Could someone else be his coach?' Gus asked.

His dad and I laughed.

'Well your dad could give it a try,' I suggested.

Gus looked at his dad. 'He wouldn't know what to do.'

'Um yes, it would be tricky coaching Sneaky Poo when he is with you at your school,' said his dad.

I had a think. 'What about if you're the boss and your dad is your sometimes helper?'

Gus, his dad and I talked for the session about Sneaky Poo, about his tricks, about how to help him remember his home. Gus and his dad marked out routes from rooms in his house to the toilet and timed how long it took Gus to get to them. Gus estimated how long this would be at school and agreed how to signal to his teacher that he was leaving for the toilet.

We looked at how his tummy might tell him that Sneaky Poo was ready for the loo and at other tricks for getting him into the toilet.

To be fair, Gus, his dad and I had many problems with Sneaky Poo. He was very tricky and it took quite a bit of practising to make sure he was safely in the toilet. But Gus' confidence grew and grew. Rather than feeling ashamed, overwhelmed, avoidant and generally stuck, he suddenly felt capable, proud and engaged. He was able to see the problem for what it was.

On the last session with Gus we reviewed our work with Sneaky Poo. I will always remember his comments. 'Knowing about Sneaky Poo has helped us all to know what to do,' Gus explained. 'I told my brother how he works and my brother is brilliant at getting his poos in the toilet now.'

'Wow, you really do know about Sneaky Poo!' I exclaimed.

Gus considered for a moment. 'Hmm, but I don't think my teacher would understand about him though.'

When a child is able to be separate from the problem, he suddenly becomes free to join forces with his parents and others around him to work out solutions. He is the clever, capable person and the problem becomes the problem.

As a parent, you are unlikely to need to tell a story as elaborate as Sneaky Poo. Nonetheless, it is very helpful to consider how you separate your child out from the problem. Small shifts in the way you talk about difficulties – being kind and collaborative, but also separating a child from the problem – allow your child to shift his perspective and gain more influence over a problem he has been avoiding.

Externalizing a difficulty often happens quite naturally with younger children. Younger children (from about four to six years old) enjoy playful discussions so you can relax more and not feel too constrained.

Tips for Collaborating with Younger Children (4–6-year-olds)

Younger children respond quickly and easily when we give a problematic behaviour or feeling a character. The possibilities are endless. I might say things such as:

- (If a child wets himself) *'Oh dear that silly old pee-pee! Let's clean it up. It can be so tricky can't it?'*
- (If a child is cross and tired) *'Ah is that grumpy feeling around again? What does it need to feel better?'*
- (If a child has made a large mess) *'Goodness, the messy monster has been here – that's quite a pile. We should teach him how to tidy that up. Let's show him how to tidy it up together.'*

Tips for Collaborating with Older Children (7–11-year-olds)

Your older child might be very comfortable with you using funny, playful characters to externalize difficult emotions and behaviours. Equally, however, they might need to know that you are respecting their more grown-up selves by using more serious language.

One way of doing this is to talk about the problem as part of something like the brain:

'You had a really scary moment when you fell off your skateboard. Your brain remembers that. Because it doesn't understand how skateboards work yet, it worries that that will always happen and so it keeps being frightened. It thinks to keep you safe you need to stay away from all skateboards. It doesn't know that you just need to time to learn how to balance on one and so it's just got stuck thinking the same old thing all the time. What it needs is for you to help it feel more confident around skateboards. Let's think up a plan to show your brain that skateboards can be fun.'

If this seems to pique his interest, then you can continue with something like this:

'Now we're going to reassure your brain that we can do this and feel okay. So for this to work, you will be trying out things that might make your brain feel worried – but they will be little things so the worry is manageable. For your brain to get comfortable, it needs to know that you are in charge and that you can be trusted. If you, as the boss, feel a step is too big then we will stop, have a think and find another way. And by the end, your brain will feel a little bit surer and more comfortable.'

Just as for Gus with Sneaky Poo, as soon as a child separates from the anxiety and thinks of it as part of his brain's misunderstanding, he feels more orientated, more grounded and confident. He gets to bring in his wider understandings and abilities.

Reflective Conversations

Often when you start working to compassionately change something, your child will start thinking more about the process. When you discuss things with him, he might make requests or suggestions. In this way he acknowledges the need to keep going and he begins to take more control.

You can help guide these reflections:

- Talk through the different challenges and the different emotions and abilities he used when he was facing these.
- You might say: *'When you started, I bet if felt so hard. I felt really proud that you were feeling all those different emotions and trying to balance them all out.'*
- Pinpoint particular challenges: *'That last part was tough, and you kept going. That must have taken a lot of courage. Did you notice a feeling like that around?'*
- Reflect on what could work better (include yourself in the change).
- Ask him if there were any times when his emotions felt too big and where, in retrospect, he would have liked to have stopped for a bit to steady himself.
- Listen to his thoughts, concerns and ideas. Ask his opinion on the way forward.

5 POINTS TO REMEMBER FROM STEP 3

- **Responding compassionately to avoidance and difficulties means using kindness and connection to help a child to steady his emotions**. You help him move toward the things he values rather than pulling away and avoiding. His confidence grows and he feels more capable around emotions.

- **Addressing avoidance compassionately strengthens your child's EQ** since you're showing him how to be more emotionally agile and resourceful. He is able to slow down and steady his emotions and with your help work through difficulties.

- **When you act compassionately**:
  o You are aware that rushing your child into the avoided situation too abruptly or aggressively can act to ramp up his fears, leaving him panicking. He digs his heels in and the anxiety and avoidance become worse.
  o Instead, you acknowledge his feelings kindly and warmly. You slowly help him think about how he can begin to feel more comfortable and at ease in a situation.
  o You help him find this 'edge' by balancing kindness and support, with steady curiosity and a gentle persistence.
  o You listen carefully to his emotions and make him the expert on what he can manage.
  o You steady him so that he can access feelings of braveness and 'can-do' each time he approaches the anxious feelings.

- **Compassionate change doesn't happen in a straight line**. There will be many setbacks and difficulties. Rather than trying to completely overcome avoidance you focus helping your child steady and balance his emotions through times of change.
- **Addressing avoidance happens best when you work with your child to approach small, manageable difficulties**. Consistency, frequency and patience are key.

10

STEP 4:
INCREASE PLAYFULNESS

*'Attachment isn't just about being connected. It's
about getting a big kick out of being alive and out of
interacting with other human beings.'*
Stanley Greenspan: 1997 – The Growth of the Mind

*'Play is often talked about as if it were a relief from
serious learning. But, for children, play is serious
learning. Play is really the work of childhood.'*
Fred Rogers

Whilst emotions can seem difficult and tight, a playful approach to emotional intelligence brings a sense of relief and connection. In Step 4 you'll discover how play enables a child to process and open out tense, anxious emotions and to explore the strengths in their own ability to be vulnerable and connect. We'll look at the different ways play can be brought into your relationship with your child to help you connect and communicate but also to help her process childhood themes of powerlessness and control, anxiety, rejection and difficult/ challenging behaviours.

We were rushing out. I was hurrying around in the usual panic when my son said, in a plaintive voice, 'Mummy, why can't we have sand in the house?'

Now, we have a sandpit in the garden and have a long-standing battle with sand coming into the house, coating everything with grit – and in my rush, he did not seem to be introducing a topic of conversation that would end well. As I mentally and emotionally imagined the endless invasion of sand in the kitchen, sand in my bed, sand in the bathrooms I felt a sharp tug of irritation. Arghhh.

And then (somehow) I recognized his open, playful thought for what it was. Not a demand for a large internal sandpit. But a small invitation for connection and wondering.

'Hmm – that would be fantastic wouldn't it!' I responded.

'Yes,' he continued, 'we could fill all the upstairs with sand!'

'And water!' I followed, thinking somehow of Caribbean Island rather than the messy bedrooms.

'And, Mummy,' he gulped (putting on his shoes as I fished his hat out of a basket), 'we could have boats which we rowed around up there and sand and some rocks and… and… we could have fish.'

He continued out to the car with me, talking in the same vein, His voice cheery, engaged and energetic.

PLAY – YOUR CHILD'S LANGUAGE

Our children often live in a very different world to ours. I don't simply mean that they are more fantastical. Rather I am talking about their sense of possibility, their curiosity about things, the liveliness of their thoughts. From my adult viewpoint (which can be full of obstacles and difficulties), my son's question about sand was annoying and impractical. From his perspective, he was simply interested in chatting about a world of joyful possibilities and creativity.

A child's playful world gives her a swift, energetic way of connecting with people and ideas. In play, she is physical and whimsical. The here-and-now can be mixed with imaginary characters and events whilst she dips in and out of the everyday. My children regularly move between daydreams and normality, as though the two were one. For example, my older daughter allows herself space to believe in Father Christmas, despite her friend explaining that it is a story made up by parents. *'The whole* real *thing is actually not important,'* she announced decisively, indicating that she wanted no further discussion and returning to her book.

Although we might find the innocence and unworldliness of play sweet, it is an essential part of being human. Tom Robbins in his book *Still Life with a Woodpecker* comments:

> *'Traits such as curiosity about the world, flexibility of response, and playfulness are common to practically all young mammals but are usually rapidly lost with the onset of maturity in all but humans. Humanity has advanced, when it has advanced, not because it has been sober, responsible and cautious, but because it has been playful, rebellious and immature.'*

These characteristics and the agile, fluid responses they create are the basis for emotional intelligence and intelligence in general.

Childhood can be a time of powerlessness. Children are littler, weaker, less respected, less skilled and less able to influence events. In an effort to deal with this they can become either overly focused on enacting emotions that feel powerful and controlling, or the opposite – they become trapped by anxiety, needing constant reassurance.

PLAYFULNESS AND EQ

One of the key components of emotional intelligence is the ability to be psychologically flexible. That is the capacity to be spontaneous, responsive and agile. When you play with your child you create a space away from tight, fearful emotions. You and your child investigate and examine and recreate situations. The 'pretend' space that is created helps her to become less self-conscious, less doubtful, and fuller hearted.

Although a child won't necessarily recognize the similarities between play and the real world, her emotions do. When situations that call for these emotions are played out, your child reflects on these emotions from within a protected, safe space. From this protected space her emotions slow down and orientate, they move from aggressive, defensive responses back to more open, connected emotions. Importantly, the next time these emotions come up in the real world, she can slow down and reconnect with the safety and balance she experienced through play.

When you play with your child, it's essential that she feels connected to you and safe. A child who feels comfortable and secure in her play will take more risks, she explores more, shifting emotionally and thinking through different perspectives. Because of these shifts she learns to reflect on situations with greater agility and capacity. Her capacity for play helps her to process social situations and difficulties and to regulate tight, distressed emotions. And on top of all of this, she has great fun.

PLAYFULNESS AND EMOTIONALLY HEALTHY ENVIRONMENTS

Adults generally think of play as something that happens between children. A friend told me that his father always kept away when he was young and only began engaging with him when they had (and this is my friend quoting him) 'finished with being tiresome and playful'. I always thought this a great shame since children thrive emotionally when their relationships with the adults are built on a range of interactions: warm, loving, connected and safe; but also excited, amused, thoughtful, silly and passionate.

Psychologist Allan Schore, working in the field of emotions and attachment, points out that robust, joyful interactions with parents create an emotionally healthy 'background state'. Just as a child will become chronically over-aroused if the parent is too emotionally intrusive and insensitive, so too, if a child doesn't have sufficient access to more positive, expressive relationships, she risks developing a low or possibly depressed emotional baseline (Schore, 2015).

When parents relate playfully to a child, she experiences a background of richer, engaged emotions. This playful, warm background speaks to safety and security. She learns to feel comfortable and safe with emotions. She can practise being excited, aroused, interested, fearful, irritable – all within a frame of comfort, love and security.

PLAYFULLY CONNECTING

For children, play is the gateway to processing emotions and there is no better way to learn about emotions than through *you*. Playing with an emotionally responsive adult allows a child to learn many skills that she can't access through peer play. She learns how to negotiate, how to lose, how to judge a play situation. If children don't have the opportunity to practise playing with a responsive adult, they find it hard to be free and spontaneous. They become distressed when they lose, and play shifts becoming focused on enacting power and control.

HOW TO INCREASE PLAYFULNESS: KEY SKILLS

BECOME MORE PLAYFUL WHEN YOU AREN'T SURE HOW

Being playful with your child can feel like a lot of effort at first. The problem is, so does a bored, anxious, disconnected child – and the exertion involved in playfulness is far more liberating. In being playful you realize how intensely engaged and resourceful your child can be. A quiet, distant child often does an about-turn, becoming engaged and enthused with ideas. Her appetite for more involved exploration seems to unlock. So, how can we bring that playfulness into our interactions with our child?

When I was a child, my parents were friends with an old colonel. He lived on his own. I remember his apartment smelling of coffee. I also remember the eye-wateringly sweet fudge he made (which my mum always hid from us). Being a colonel, he was very serious. He sat talking to my mum but wouldn't talk to us until we leant over and pressed his nose. 'Honk!' said the colonel. It was loud. To our glee, he acted as if it hadn't happened.

He was similarly surprising in the garden. If we were playing, he would make his way through the grass on his hands and knees with no small amount of dignity. With a straight face he would wait for us to notice. Of course, we loved it and were soon climbing on his back, pressing his nose, rubbing our grubby hands through his hair.

Looking back, his key play skills seemed to centre on these two talents: honking when we pressed his nose and crawling around on hands and knees.

Making Play Small and Easy

The easiest way to increase your confidence around play is to realize how often you play with your children anyway. There have likely been many times when you and your child had a playful interaction. When she was young you perhaps spoke with her teddies, ate her playdough cakes and as she got older, chased her, and sung or danced with her.

The fact is, our children are constantly inviting us to be playful. Did your child ever go through a 'Why?' phase? It took me years to realize it was an invitation to connect.

When my son was young I spent many an hour answering 'Why?' questions until one day I asked him playfully, 'Why are you asking "Why?"?'

He replied: ''Cos that's the way it goes.'

I quickly learnt my lesson. The next time he asked me 'Why?', rather than trotting out a long worthy answer I would reply, 'Because the sky is a beautiful green colour today and we are frogs!' Or 'Because Daddy is off on a secret space mission and only you and I can know.'

On occasion, my son became annoyed and then I knew he really wanted an answer, but most of the time he would laugh and ask another impossible question. I was saved from exhaustingly explaining abstract details and we had great fun.

Lawrence Cohen in *Playful Parenting* calls these small moments 'playful interludes'. They are the kinds of interactions that happen without too much thought or direction. Scattered throughout the day, they give both you and your child a sense of security and wellbeing, relaxation and connection.

Here are some ideas for small and easy play:

- If you're feeling particularly low on energy and definitely not up for a full-on play session, settle yourself on the floor near your child as she plays. She soon spies you out of the corner of her eye but your entry into playfulness is allowed to be lazy and slow and unadventurous. The demand feels less, which allows playful ideas to surface.
- Playful 'what-if' discussions are great when you are out on walks. You might say, *'What if that tree was made of chocolate and we could go over there and take a big chunk?'* Or *'What if my legs grew really long and we could get anywhere really quickly. Where would we go?'*
- Develop your own playful routines. For example, arrange your child's soft toys in the bedroom so that when it's time for bed the children find 'big bear' driving a tiny car, or 'rabbit' organizing a toy procession. You child will love coming up the stairs to find out what the toys have been up to. Of course, you'll deny any knowledge of these strange goings-on.

Rather than playing for your child's sake, see if you can find a way to play just to be present and share time. Take the pressure out and be dreamy and low energy if you need.

This background playfulness builds up a sense of connection, competence and trust between you and your child. With this as your foundation, not only is there more trust and warmth in your relationship, but it also becomes easier to respond resourcefully and playfully when your child is experiencing difficulty.

WHEN IT'S DIFFICULT TO CONNECT WITH YOUR CHILD

> 'He drew a circle that shut me out –
> Heretic, rebel, a thing to flout.
> But Love and I had the wit to win:
> We drew a circle that took him in!'
> A.S. Neill

A little girl I knew, Cerys, had a stream of imaginary friends popping in called 'Bills'. They lived in a very complex, sophisticated land where all the Bills had differently coloured babies (green, yellow, red) and had to do what the police told them. The ruler of this land was a king who was also a policeman and also best friends with Blue Baby Bill.

The descriptions were very detailed, very complex and, to be frank, very constant. Her brother, Ed, also had a kingdom, but his realm was much more dynamic and he (rather than a policeman with a colourful baby) was the supreme ruler. 'I will blast your head off!' he would shout as I tried to drink my coffee.

Listening at full-pelt to the story of the Bills was often mentally exhausting. But then, having my head blasted off by a supreme ruler at every turn was physically gruelling. Try as I might, conversations with Cerys had a habit of returning to the Bills and it seemed repetitive and intense ('*Do you think he'd like a Violet or Pink Haze baby, Anne?*'). With Ed, the supreme ruler, there was far less conversation and far more head blasts.

Now, I have no problem with a child having her own time to play quietly alone or even charging around with friends in a state of parallel play. But sometimes, a child and her parents begin to be very separate. Your child might struggle to relate to the gentler, slower, meandering conversations that you find more comfortable. But similarly, you find her boisterous, physically charged games or her complicated, intricate worlds excluding and difficult to engage with.

In helping a child to connect to us emotionally, we have to first be able to connect with her. Through our receptivity and attention, she becomes more aware of the relationship and of us. She comes to directly understand what it means to respond to and accommodate another person and how meaningful and fun this can be.

My friend Amos helped me a great deal when it came to the shoot-'em-up types of game.

Amos had a relaxed, easy way with his grandchildren. He seemed to be able to engage with whatever came up. I remember him playing with a grandchild who suddenly ambushed him, eyes steely, shouting, 'I'm blasting your head off!' On being ambushed, Amos crashed back dramatically from his chair, shouting, 'Oh no! Could it be? I think so... Yes, my head has been blown off!'

His grandchild, slightly taken back by the success of his shot, paused – but Amos continued, 'Now where is my super-powerful fart gun? A fart gun so powerful, even the clouds run for cover.' (Grandchild begins readying himself to shoot Amos again.)

'If I just press this trigger...' He turns his finger which is acting as the fart gun so that he is sticking it in his own face. He pulls the trigger and then he falls to the ground again.

Amos' grandchild would start laughing, as would Amos.

Amos' ability to join in and have fun without having to be the dominant gun-blaster created a shift in the play. It allowed his grandson to see that it's okay to be vulnerable. That fun can be had from being helpless as well as powerful. Most importantly, he learnt that his grandfather wanted to join with him, that his play made sense and that they could connect and relate to each other.

Swearing and Insults – Fat Farty Farty Face

Some behaviours feed off our horrified or offended responses. Swearing is a good example of this. I've found that when a child swears or throws out insults, parents get tied in knots. On the one hand, they feel that they should ignore bad language – after all, the reaction these words provoke feed into the excitement. But on the other hand, they want to step in and act, rather than allowing a child to be so rude.

This is where playfulness helps. When we take a playful approach to swearing or insults, we take the power out of the words. Rather than leaving a child feeling powerful but isolated, her words are met with humour and confidence – much more steadying emotions. Let me give an example from my household.

My nine-year-old daughter has a tight-knit group of friends and there is much discussion at school around what it means to be kind. My daughter will often come home telling me of some 'unkind' thing a child has said and the girls' efforts to comfort each other. This had an impact at home when our son, who is two years younger called her a fathead. Having never before been aware that the word fat could be considered a critical word, she suddenly becomes activated: 'That's so rude!' she scolds. 'It's very mean to call someone fat.'

Her brother's interest suddenly switches on. One of the many silly things he'd said each day for goodness knows how long had caused a reaction: 'Fat, fat, fat!' he called out joyfully. I could see where this was heading so I decided to interrupt.

'No – no – not fat!' I moaned in mock dismay, pretending he had been aiming this at me. 'Could it be my rather large feet? Or maybe my ear? I've often felt my earlobe was rather porky...This is a dreadful situation! – Well you're... you're... you're... a farty nin-kom-pooper – so there!'

At this, my son burst out laughing. My daughter shook her head dismissively and returned to her drawing.

As I write this, I can imagine parents worrying that such a reaction would only encourage rude and potentially upsetting behaviour and I can see their concern. It is of course important that a child learns which behaviours are socially acceptable and which aren't. When I initially play this, the child will get excited and play out silly statements more. But importantly, the behaviour is no longer creating a disconnection. If any further insults happen later, I can say (with far more connection, softness and influence), 'Stop now, you know we can't use those words because they are not said in a nice way. We were having a bit of fun earlier but it's not something we say if it hurts feelings.'

It is as if the playfulness comes in and reframes the difficult, tense behaviour. Rather than being seen as emotionally spiteful or nasty, it is seen in a different light. It becomes a funny mistake that couldn't possibly have had any real wicked intent. And since being oppositional and defiant can feel lonely and difficult, your child can quickly take your lead with this, going along with the play, relieved of the burden of their bad behaviour.

A NOTE ON DIFFICULT AND CHALLENGING BEHAVIOUR

What about behaviours which are dangerous and challenging? Sometimes a child's behaviour is more challenging and potentially dangerous. She might have thrown an object hard, hurt a sibling or damaged something important. These behaviours tighten play and stop a child shifting and playing in a more emotionally connected manner.

When a child's behaviour has stepped over the line and has become dangerous or damaging, engaging with her playfully will just confuse her and prevent her from understanding boundaries and safety.

First things first, you help contain and prevent dangerous hurtful behaviours. *'Come over here with me, I can't let you throw X/hurt Y.'*

When the storm is over and she has had plenty of time to relax and recharge, you might say playfully: *'There were some big big feelings and behaviours there. Do you feel okay now?' What do you think was going on? It felt like a super mega storm!'* Of course, with older or younger children you change the language to adapt to their sensibilities or understandings.

The point in these slightly more playful interactions is to make it clear that the normal *'You did wrong, there will be consequences'* conversation is not your main concern or interest. Rather, you want to bring a playful energy into naming the emotions behind behaviours, and through that lens find a more comfortable, easy way to reflect.

PLAYFUL REPAIRS

Our relationship with our child is constantly shifting and reforming. We looked at this in chapters 4 and 5 when we explored Good Enough Parenting and Emotional Repairs

Breaks or disruptions in relationship with a parent are instinctively stressful for a child. Children want to repair these breaks, and play gives them a way. The problem is that repairs can become very difficult for an adult, let alone a child to do, through the normal language-based route (an apology requires a lot of reflection and maturation – it also insists that one party was right and the other wrong). A far more natural and possible way forward is through a 'playful repair'.

At around seven and ten years of age, my older sister and I often argued and fought. Sometimes to such a degree that my great aunt, who lived upstairs, would come out of her room with her frying pan in hand. She thought the noise was intruders. Anyway, as the older one, my sister was aware that we were likely to get into trouble if there was too much noise. To calm things down, she had a short routine that worked every time.

Typically, there would have been a stormy argument which would either be running out of energy or in danger of turning bad. I would be planning my next move (telling Mum/going and messing up her bed) when my sister would look at me out of the corner of her eye. Slowing, she would begin miming turning on a tap. 'Just running my bath,' she'd say.

Now this might seem an odd way to behave, when we had just been having a full-blown argument but it was a well-developed ritual between us. It signalled the beginning of a repair.

As soon as my sister began 'running her bath', I would feel waves of relief.

'Now whatever you do,' my sister would continue, 'don't take the plug out.' And there was my in. With a shy smile I would go over and pull the imaginary plug whilst my sister enacted outrage and fluster.

I clearly remember the feeling of relief as the tension from the argument turned into a playful release. My whole body seemed to let go and then, I would begin laughing and laughing. Of course, I would insist that my sister ran her bath again and we would repeat, but importantly I would have achieved my 'moment in charge'. Things felt comfortable and safe.

Playful Repairs in Practice

Repairing yourself, then repairing things with your child. When the sheer demands of life make you feel grumpy and limited, a playful comment to your child can lighten your mood. I might say to one of my children, *'Can you help me? I've got a head full of grumps and busyness.'* My children are normally only too willing to help. This simple act helps me to hold my emotions more lightly and also gives my children the chance to see that I am fully human and can need help to wind down.

Repairing when you and your child are stuck in battles over little things. Routine tasks such as tidying up, getting changed or brushing teeth can often attract little frustrations. Take a playful and silly approach to repair repetitive flare-ups. If a child won't tidy up with you, begin putting things away in the wrong place. Perhaps put teddy bears in the fridge, cars in plant pots and craft stuff under a cushion. When she won't brush her teeth, another regularly used playful tactic is to pretend to scrub the door, floors and sink with the toothbrush. Inevitably your child will start laughing at this behaviour. The hard feelings dissolve, the job gets done and your relationship is repaired.

If a more significant upset has occurred with a child, then make sure you start a repair carefully and tentatively. You can start by offering a space for a chat. Sometimes a child will say, *'But you were really horrible to me,'* or *'I felt really bad.'* If you need to apologize, then do this readily and openly. Offer a cuddle and then a play repair can happen. Our family favourites are Amos' fart guns and a bit of playful wrestling.

USE PLAYFULNESS TO HELP FEELINGS OF POWERLESSNESS AND DIFFERENCE

Playfulness provides a background sense of stability, connection and repair. However, there are likely to be times that call out for more thoughtful play. Perhaps interactions between you and your child that have become difficult and tense. Your child may be having particular difficulties (say with schoolwork or with friends). Or it could be that she is experiencing a period of change (new school, family death or separation). At these times, purposefully creating more playful space and connection helps your child to process these difficult experiences. Let's look at some examples of how play helps work through some of these difficult emotional tangles.

I met Arlo when he was ten. He was receiving in-patient treatment for a range of complex physical conditions. A side effect of one of his conditions was that his appetite was hard to manage and he had become seriously overweight.

The medical team gave strict instructions around Arlo's diet and the cook at the residential unit spent a lot of time designing 'healthier' meals to fit with this. Unfortunately, Arlo was always thinking about mealtimes. Throughout the day he could smell the food being cooked. When it was finally time for a meal, he was first into the canteen, gulping down his food within a couple of minutes, then waiting in a state of agitated eagerness for pudding.

Arlo's 'special' pudding was not the regular one. In line with the medical team's guidance, the cook would have prettily arranged a pudding of sliced fruit and little scoops of sorbet, but Arlo just wanted the hot sponge puddings he saw all around. Gazing at the puddings, his bottom lip stuck out and large tears made their way down his cheeks. 'I want the real pudding not this!' he sobbed.

The situation often played on my mind. The unit was too small to hide the fact that all sorts of great-smelling things were being cooked for the others – we had tried to sit in a separate room with him but with the travelling smell, he nonetheless became very upset. His awareness of food and restrictions only seemed to be increasing.

One afternoon, after lunch, a surprise opportunity to play things through presented itself. I was sitting with Arlo in the main lounge and a younger child came up to give me a plate of playdough cakes.

Arlo looked at the plate and then at the child serving me. 'Unfortunately, Anne is on a special diet,' he announced. 'She can only eat books today.'

'What!' I exclaimed, in mock outrage.

'Yes, sorry, Anne. Just books for you, and only really old ones.'

I did my best impression of John McEnroe. 'You cannot be serious!' I cried. 'I want the delicious and scrumptious green playdough cakes, not the dry old books!'

At my response, Arlo howled with laughter. The other children, seeing the fun, laughed too. We continued to play this out for quite a while. Arlo was the ringleader but the other children also joined in to find more and more boring, inedible items for my snack. The other staff members were enjoying the spectacle.

We spoke about it in the team meeting. It was clear that through playing out my book eating, Arlo had found a way to process the feelings of difference and powerlessness. What's more, he was obviously loving being part of the group again. In this game, I was the different one, and Arlo could join with the others. His sense of relief felt immense.

'Why don't you play this out during lunch?' suggested one of my colleagues. It had the potential to be a bit raucous, but the situation as it stood was tight and awful. It was decided that I would sit in the dining room and have my lunch. When it came to pudding, I would be served a pile of books.

The game worked a treat. My colleague sat with Arlo and egged him on whilst he called out to the others, 'Sadly, Anne has a very very boring book to eat for pudding today.' I made suitably sorrowful, grumpy and sometimes disbelieving faces as newly boring books arrived for me to eat. The joy and relief on Arlo's face as I became the focus of attention was blissful. He began to pay very little attention to his own pudding, such was his enjoyment of the game.

As children get older, they are keenly aware of both being treated differently and of things not being within their control. For Arlo, his health difficulties separated him out. He had little control over his appetite and over the decisions made to reduce his calorie intake. Although the particulars of Arlo's situation are more unusual, children often experience being different or feeling marginalized and powerless.

A child might feel excluded or lack control around friends. There may be family changes such as separation or new siblings. She could be struggling academically or socially. Even when a child's life is relatively stable, feelings of powerlessness and invisibility are a common theme. When you reverse the power in play, your child can step away from the feelings and reflect. The laughter lets go of the tension and the tight, painful emotions shift.

When Power and Control are Exerted in Play
Given the regularity and quantity of unsettling, unbalancing experiences, a child can struggle when she doesn't have a

playful reflective space to discharge fear and anxiety and reconnect to others. She might discover that she can overcome the powerlessness and lack of control by exerting her own authority and control over others. The contrast between her background feeling of being out of control and the feeling when she is the one who calls the shots feels good. It acts as a quick, effective relief from the vulnerable feelings she had before. We see this when children are challenging in their behaviour or when younger children have tantrums or refuse everything.

Unfortunately, without lots of opportunity to explore and open out what it feels like to be powerful through play, a child can turn to habitually controlling others in order to shift her own difficult feelings. I'm thinking of the child who seems to want to exert control over friends at school. The child who will, for example, tease, control or exclude another child.

Ignoring for a moment the impact of this behaviour on the excluded child, the child who exerts control pushes away feelings which feel uncomfortable and doesn't get to release tension around her initial feelings of powerlessness. She is stuck in a repetitive cycle of passing on the original feelings of exclusion and powerlessness. Furthermore, the repetitive tight nature of this behaviour can hinder her in developing more empathic and compassionate relationships.

'Playing Out' Powerlessness

Although the many smaller daily injustices, confusions and discomforts can't be avoided, 'playing out' experiences of exclusion or powerlessness helps a child's emotions to rebalance and shift. She lets go of some of the tension she feels around her own experiences and sees them with greater perspective.

'Playing out' means reflecting on things that have been difficult. When she plays out situations, instead of feeling isolated and powerless, she discovers a way to engage more with her experiences whilst also feeling a greater connection to others. So:

- The laughter invited by play dissolves the fear and tension and your child can slowly begin reflecting on her experiences. The connection to others dismisses the lurking feeling of being alone, powerless or different.
- Whilst many interactions between parents and children are hierarchical, play researchers describe playful interactions as horizontal (Lindsay and Mize, 2000), meaning there is more equality and shared input. In the context of a child's feelings of powerlessness and exclusion, this collaborative play helps her to experience and understand equality and shared power.
- Furthermore, while playing with you, a child comes to understand the joy and connection that exists in a more equal relationship. She directly experiences the difference between collaborative behaviours and those that are unequal and controlling. In this way, creativity, collaboration and connection have the space to outshine her need to control and dominate others.

Playful Skills for When Your Child Feels Powerless
Reverse play around separations (particularly good for under-fives).

When she was about two or three years old my daughter loved pretending to leave me. 'Bye, bye, Mama, I got to go,' she would say breezily as we walked down the road. She would then hide behind a lamppost whilst I stood pretend sobbing. 'Oh no, do you have to go!' I would wail.

Children starting nursery or school love these types of reversals. My daughter was never particularly upset at being left at nursery, but she still loved the game. Over and over we would play 'Bye, Mummy.'

There are many variations of this reversing roles. For example, when a child has become concerned about food and is refusing to eat a range of foods, you can reverse roles and pretend to be very timid in your eating choices. Although it might sound like this is teasing or mocking a child, it actually works to give your child some room for reflection on their difficulty.

> One child I did this with giggled so much when I showed great apprehension over a carrot that she got the hiccups. She quickly recovered herself and then enacted a very adult like, no-nonsense position. 'Carrots are really very normal and nothing to be at all worried about,' she told me with authority (even though up until this point she had refused to eat anything other than beige food). She then demonstrated how easy it would be to eat carrots as if this had never been a difficulty for her. Her mother's eyes popped out.

Role playing when your child is being left out by friends (eight years and under). Sometimes a child responds better to a puppet game where you can role play a similar situation. For example, if your child has had difficulties at school and has been feeling left out, then use one of her toys (a soft animal works well) to role play. This often works best if it seems to occur naturally.

You might notice a soft toy and comment, 'I think rabbit is feeling left out by all the other animals.' If your child seems interested or responsive you can ask her questions about the rabbit. 'I'm not sure exactly what's been happening with rabbit. Do you know? How does rabbit feel? What does she need?' Sometimes you'll be surprised at how simple the answer can be – 'Little rabbit needs a cuddle and a game with her brothers' – although not always: ('Little rabbit's dad is going to go and tell those girls off!').

Role playing to help a child reflect on their own controlling behaviour. When children experience difficulty with feelings of powerlessness they can become tense and their behaviour can become difficult and provoking. As they get older this tension can come out in controlling behaviour toward friends. If you think your child is acting out more powerful behaviours, then play gives her the opportunity to reflect on these.

- Get a group of toys (can be dolls, teddies, cars, trucks) and pretend that they are leaving another of the toys out.
- Ask your child how the left-out toy might be feeling. Ask her if it can feel exciting for the children leaving the child out (this might sound strange, but it acknowledges the real payoff in these behaviours).
- Ask if there are any other good games that are still exciting but that all the animals can play together. Remember this is play – the idea is to keep opening out her ideas rather than telling her how to think.
- If she says things you think need challenging then you can try, '*I'm not sure about that. I think better games happen when everyone plays.*'

Playfully responding to 'mean' behaviour. Power play doesn't have to be unusual or negative. Rather, it can be very common in children, particularly when they've experienced many situations where they have less control. When his daughter says something mean, a friend has a funny tactic. He sweeps her up with the words: '*Oh no! Those naughty, naughty Meanies. Listen to what they're saying. I'm going to have to shake them out. Come on, Meanies, show yourselves!*' whilst he jiggles his laughing daughter up and down.

Responding to your child's behaviour with direct, engaged whole-heartedness not only maintains your connection with her but – funnily enough – you also teach her about behaviour. Having learnt about 'meanness' in the above context, a child is likely to play around a bit at being mean just to have a few more turns at being jiggled, but whilst she does this, she is recognizing and sorting mean behaviours.

Playing through different forms of 'meanness' develops her understanding. When she sees meanness in others, she is empowered to call it out, give it a name, feel engaged and capable. She learns that tense emotions can be expressed meanly but they can also be worked through playfully. She is reminded that the joy of connection is far more rewarding then the short-term appeal of meanness.

Reversing roles: allowing your child to be a baby. Sometimes, children work so hard to feel big and in control that it can feel like a great relief and comfort to be able to be a baby for a while. Try the game 'naughty baby'. In this game siblings can be brought in to try and look after the naughty baby and your child gets to be wilful and carefree and silly, but also cherished and soothed. The burden of being 'grown up' and responsible is eased. I've often also found that a child will allow herself to become softer and more vulnerable and open after the game.

PLAYFUL SKILLS FOR ANXIETY

We've already looked at how children can enact feelings of powerlessness or exclusion by acting to control and exclude others. When a child feels overwhelmed, her response might not be to enact control over others; rather it might be to turn in on herself, becoming anxious and apprehensive, and to control these feelings by avoidance.

We saw this in Step 3 when we looked at leading with compassion. Feelings of anxiety switch a child's body into a stressful, fight-or-flight state. She can become locked into this fear response and conversations around safety and security become tense and counterproductive. Whilst it's important to help a child to manage and work through this avoidance, a playful approach can work behind the scenes to reduce her sense of shame and overwhelm.

When a child is anxious or avoiding situations, playfulness allows a child's emotions to slow. The play sets a tone of safety and security: Giggling and laughter release tension and a child re-establishes a sense of safety and control. Her body is regulated and comfortable. *'The danger is over,'* she tells her brain. *'I am back in a safe place.'*

Reversing Roles

Children who are experiencing anxiety find it a great relief to see themes around anxiety played out in a light-hearted way by a parent. They get to be the fearless one, the one who knows what to do, the one who calms *you* down.

You might be walking along the road when you discover that you're very frightened of the cracks in the paving. If she responds with giggles then you've likely hit on some tight feelings. Look to hold her hand for reassurance, ask her what you can do if a bear jumps out. Hide behind her, keep stumbling over your feet.

Bedtime Anxiety

Children often get anxious around bedtime (perhaps they worry about monsters, or for older children, the idea of intruders creates tension). Sometimes it's clear what has triggered this but often it's hard to work this out.

When a child gets anxious at bedtime it can be very healthy for her to play around with the idea of safety (and to consider what constitutes braveness and courage). A great favourite with the families I work with is a game called 'Teddies On Guard'. I get parents and children to collect all teddies from around the house (if the child is bigger this may mean a dig around the attic for toys that have been grown out of!). Then each teddy is given a specific duty. Giraffe can guard the stairs; Green Alien, the toilet. The child goes around the house putting teddies into the place they need to guard. Parents can play games with this by pretending that Dog is a bit scared on his own or that Cow thinks he is a superhero. Your child gets to project her feels of anxiety onto some of the animals, but also her braveness onto others. She also begins to associate the house with a loving, secure playfulness rather than danger or uncertainty.

Specific Anxieties

Specific anxieties are anxieties around a thing or a situation. A playful approach doesn't try too hard to get rid of a child's fear. Rather, it seeks to take the sting out of that fear instead. If the anxiety is relatively small or new you can be silly and overtly playful. You might say: *'Those ridiculously dreadful spiders, planning the downfall of the human race. I wouldn't put up with it.'* Equally, you can play around, replacing a reaction of fear with fun dynamic play. Here are some ideas for playing through mild anxiety with a specific focus:

If a child has a specific anxiety around injections, certain vegetables, spiders or dirt you can use these to create a playful remedy. Insert the word magic in front of the thing she is worried about (magic shots, magic tomatoes, magical dirt).

You can represent the feared thing using, for example, a toy syringe from a doctor's set, a wooden tomato from a play kitchen or some dried black beans for dirt.

In hushed tones, tell your child that you have in your possession a magic syringe/tomato etc. Give yourself an injection, hug the tomato, run his hands through the 'dirt' and see what magical powers are passed on.

The magical object might give the power to fly, it could make you very very heavy, or turn everyone else invisible…

WHEN ANXIETY IS BIG

When a child's anxiety looms large, it's important not to retrigger fears or push a child into areas where things feel tighter and less playful. General play is important since a loving, comfortable, easy environment helps her to unwind and switch her focus. You might lightly reverse roles and play more worried characters but let her lead, staying away from anything that relates closely to her anxiety and being ready to stop and start as she dictates.

If Your Child Feels Ashamed or Humiliated by her Anxiety

Some anxieties receive a lot of attention and children get very self-conscious:

- If your child is very aware of an anxiety, she will quickly pull back from anything that reminds her of it. Make sure any play is steered completely free of the real fear.
- Use your instinct. If you sense your child feels belittled or teased, be swift with your apology and change direction.
- Don't attempt to draw similarities between play and her anxieties to her attention. Her brain is making the connections – your attempts will tighten her play.

TOO OLD FOR PLAY?

Children are extraordinarily playful when they are very small. The magic and mystery present in the life of a two, three and four-year-old can't be beaten. As children grow they get more verbally capable. They remember more, they recognize contexts and can adapt their explanations to the listener. The amazingly playful space they once occupied can seem far away. But don't be fooled. Don't imagine your child is too old for play when she hits seven, ten or even twelve. Older children can get cross and fed up with certain playful responses, but it would be a mistake to assume that they don't need playfulness.

Sometimes one area of playfulness begins to grate (fart guns can only work for so long). But others can be frequently fished out. I know many a nine-year-old who likes to be babied (and who will play along) happily. I have worked with numerous 12-year-olds who have greatly valued a roundup of teddies to help guard a bedroom, and why would any child *not* want to be the expert when their adult is having an anxiety attack around a cushion she thinks might be alive?

Whichever way your child reacts, put *connection* with her as the top priority. If she doesn't want playful role plays or your amateur dramatics then connect through stories, playful questions and imaginings. Balance out playfulness with discussions and more concrete reflections.

PLAYING AND STEPPING AWAY FROM PLAY

As we get to the end of this step, it's important to make a distinction between the type of open, creative, joyful play that heals and repairs emotions and the so-called playful responses that in reality act to push away or undermine emotions. For example, you might have someone in your life who seeks to make a joke at the slight sign of discomfort or vulnerable emotions, or remember a relative who tried too quickly to play when you were upset as a child. True playfulness between a parent and a child isn't an avoidance, a dismissal or a denial of sadness, upset or distress. It is connected and responsive and kind. If your child is sad, panicky or upset then hold off the play and stay connected to her emotions.

By taking the time to sooth and comfort her you let her orientate and feel your presence. Her nervous system settles, and she is able to recoup her strength. Once she has fully felt your sensitivity and support, she will feel a natural readiness for play. But importantly, the play comes *after* the acceptance and soothing.

In a similar vein, although there is a lot of wriggle room with play, it is important that you maintain a connection and responsiveness to your child's verbal and non-verbal signals. Sometimes, a parent's attempts to play frustrate a child. When she doesn't want to play, be gentle and give her space. There are many times and many ways to interact playfully – pushing her is counterproductive and doesn't respect her needs.

When you notice she is pulling back or saying *no,* being quick to respond and respect her limits preserves the collaboration and joy that is so important in play.

If your child is not good at stating her limits then a good rule of thumb is to notice whether she is engaged, giggling, coming up with hundreds of suggestions; whether she is relaxed and open, or whether she is withdrawing. Sometimes you get a very clear 'yes' from a child – her reaction is intense and quick. At other times you might feel doubtful. If this is the case, then check it out with her. Prioritize her feelings and voice.

A Note on Tickling
Although my children love being tickled, I often hold back on this and let them tickle each other. Tickling can feel overwhelming for a child and intensify feelings of powerlessness. Real playfulness is a collaborative engagement of energy and ideas.

RITUALS FOR WINDING-DOWN PLAY

Some play has a natural arc. Engagement and excitement slowly build up, there is a good deal of play and then the energy tails and children relax and unwind. But sometimes, when a child is particularly hungry for our attention, she can find it hard to let go of the play. Unfortunately, this can lead to an adult becoming frustrated and cross and the lightness and connection is lost.

If this happens, think about having a wind-down ritual. After the normal *'I am exhausted,'* I might say, *'and I need a big glass of water. Let's go into the kitchen really, really, quietly.'*

Now of course, a very playful child will take that as a cue for loud, crashing moves but nonetheless you are clearly signalling your move into a quieter time. I then slowly drink my water, shifting play to chat and thinking with the child perhaps about the washing or getting the dinner done or having some down-time. All this allows your child to reorientate and settle herself to the change.

5 POINTS TO REMEMBER FROM STEP 4

- **Play opens up your emotional connection to your child. You learn to enjoy each other and emotions ease and open out**. When you play your child feels close and connected to you. Tight emotions relating to fear, separation of shame melt away. She feels included in your world. She comes to know that her ideas, thoughts and emotional responses create happiness and connection.

- **Through play your child communicates more freely**. It's the place where she feels most confident and secure and where her ideas can be expressed. Play communicates comfort and safety where language can distance and complicate issues. It brings a lightness and ease with emotions and a connectedness with your child.

- **Play doesn't have to be big or involved**. It can be simple and small and low energy and over in a few minutes, or much, much more elaborate. And it doesn't have to seem to be about emotions for it to help a child open up emotionally.

- **Your child uses play to work through emotions**. When she plays through her experiences her emotions rebalance and shift. She can re-enact difficult experiences and investigate different emotional responses:
  - When she feels powerless, she explores what it feels like to take back control.
  - Where she has felt isolated she can reconnect to you and those around her.
  - With upset or hurt emotions, play brings understanding and emotional repair.
  - When there has been anxiety, she can explore feeling brave and strong.
  - If she feels ashamed she can take a bold, open stance through play

- **Play celebrates vulnerability and openness and all the space between**. In play, adults can reverse roles with a child, allowing the child to be the powerful one whilst taking on her experiences of vulnerability. Through stepping away from her experiences, she can reflect on them more. She learns that her own vulnerability can be understood by others and that it doesn't need to be covered up when she is with those she trusts.

11

STEP 5:
'CONTAIN' AND CONNECT
TO DIFFICULT EMOTIONS

In Step 5 we look at containing and connecting to the difficult, controlling emotions your child experiences. The emotions that push you away and block understanding. When you act to contain big, difficult feelings, you intervene to ensure that your child is safe whilst also emotionally supporting and connecting with him. In this step I will help you slow your child's emotions, step out of conflict and allow him to understand and experience the slower, quieter emotions which help him settle and reflect.

Most of the time, a child's emotional responses are pretty low key and non-complicated. They steer him through the world. When he is frightened, he comes to you; if he experiences something interesting, he investigates; when he is energetic, he moves around and plays. He settles to routines, he merges his needs with others, adapting to demands and responding to new situations. You are his default guide. Any uncertainty is sorted through you.

Some emotional responses, the responses your child needs to keep safe or to keep away danger, are faster and stronger. Their job is to grab his attention and push him to take direct action. These 'emergency' responses don't allow much negotiation or choice as this could be dangerous. For example, if he stepped out into the road and then saw a car approaching at speed, he'd step back quickly, rather than taking time to think about alternative reactions.

The thing about these quick, strong emotions is that they can seem to hijack a child. His focus and motivation, his memory, his thinking (even his body, which becomes energized and reactive) is pulled into treating a situation as urgent and requiring defensive control. This can be tough on both the child and those around him. Rather than increasing his sense of security and safety, these types of emotional responses push others away. They intensify his struggle and, when the rush of energy has passed, he can feel lost and ashamed.

This chapter looks at how you can 'contain' these big emotions, slowing them down, making them safe and putting limits around them. 'Containing' is a term often used in therapy. When your child's emotions are contained, he feels secure and connected. You put limits around behaviours that create difficulty or seek to control situations and you move closer to him emotionally: you're more in sync with him.

Being in sync is important. Your child recognizes that you are with him and can keep him safe. Rather than allowing the emotions to create bigger gaps or breaks in the relationship, you repair the emotional connection. His emotions settle and become more responsive to the actual situation. He no longer feels cut off or ashamed.

UNCONTAINED EMOTIONS

Let me give you an example of these quick, strong emotional responses and how they affect a child when they are not sufficiently connected to and contained:

I met Otto when I was newly graduated and carrying out some research at a youth centre. Otto was ten years old.

He was having difficulty at home: his dad was ill and he was often sent to stay with relatives.

Although Otto was meant to be attending the youth club, he often came to visit me in my office, wanting to hang around and grab a biscuit or a chat. Most of the time, he was funny and resourceful, but his behaviour could also be very difficult. He would swear and take things belonging to me, throw objects and refuse to leave when I had to lock up.

I was young and inexperienced and busy. My response to Otto's behaviours was to be on it. Watching for any signs that he was misbehaving. 'Otto – don't even think about going out into that hallway,' I'd say whenever poor Otto's eyes wandered, or 'You need to sit over there and I want to see your hands.'

One day, I was walking with Otto to the centre when we met his school friend and the school friend's mum. 'Otto tells us that he likes you the best because you're the toughest worker.'

'Yeah,' agreed the friend smiling widely, 'he says you have all sorts of rules just for him.'

When they had gone Otto was quiet. 'I often think you must get bored of me telling you to stop all the time,' I said. 'Isn't it more fun to hang around with Derek in the clubhouse?'

'Nah,' said Otto casually. 'I like how you can deal with me.'

Big, difficult emotions can feel burdensome for a child. Otto's were very near to the surface and hard for him to manage. He was clever and capable but couldn't settle or get on with things. His emotions were tense, hooked and vigilant.

To cope with these big, difficult emotions, Otto's emotional reactions were strong and doggedly focused on control. This made sense. Experience had taught him that relationships were fragile and unreliable. His emotions were wired to react defensively and take action at any sign of threat. And threat for Otto was people leaving him. His emotions would do whatever they could to stop people moving out of his life, but they were working overtime, reacting to the smallest sign of a problem and demanding immediate action.

The cruel thing was that rather than having the effect of strengthening Otto's relationships, his emotional reactions were pushing real friends away. In truth, Otto was being weighed down by emotional responses. And so, on those evenings after school, rather than having fun with Derek, Otto would bring himself to me.

A PARENT'S STRUGGLE TO CONTAIN EMOTIONS

Just as children struggle to manage their emotions, so too do the adults who care for them. Emotions are contagious, particularly the emotions felt by someone you love. When your child is disorientated and off balance, because you love him and care deeply, you pick up on his anguish and uncertainty. You feel both fearful and anxious, but also hooked in and angry.

Sometimes, parents respond to these emotions by becoming more authoritarian and controlling. They might find themselves thinking: 'He's doing this to control me,' or 'He needs to know that he's not in charge.' These strong thoughts feel productive in the moment. Parents feel fired up and determined to stop the behaviour, to take control and sort things out. In this emotional state, their responses are quick, cross and reflexive. They rely on their anger to carry the situation through, and their behaviour is tight and authoritarian. In the heat of the moment they might threaten big punishments, maybe they become physically dominant and loud, or maybe steely and cold.

At other times parents find themselves feeling exhausted and demoralized. They haven't got the energy to keep battling with a child, and they worry that they will further distress him, so they accommodate to the controlling behaviours. Stepping away from confrontation, they try and pacify the emotions by allowing their child to take control.

And then many parents waver between these two responses.

Unfortunately, when a parent tries to impose reflexive control (whilst emotionally feeling out of control and frustrated) instead of steadying and slowing a child's emotions, they end up further reducing his sense of competence and capability. The child either tries harder to re-exert control or shuts down and pulls away.

Equally, when a parent doesn't respond to contain or sort things out, a child is left feeling fearful and disorientated and so he keeps trying to take control. His emotions take up a lot of space and energy and other quieter, more reflective emotions are pushed out.

YOUR CHILD'S FEELINGS OF SHAME ABOUT EMOTIONS

Alongside this struggle for control, something else happens in these parent–child interactions that has a profound effect on the child. The child begins to feel ashamed of his emotional reactions. He notices that although his initial reactions seem to be strong and determined, they cause difficulties and isolate him. He is left feeling chaotic and unsure and begins to lose confidence in himself. I remember this very keenly from when I was a child and struggled with tight, strong emotional reactions around food.

It started when I was very small. I had been a very podgy baby. My legs were fat, my arms were fat and I had a fat tummy. On top of this, I was not very active. I liked to bum-shuffle but definitely wasn't interested in walking. The health visitors were concerned. They told my mum that she was feeding me too much and that my weight was getting in the way of my walking. She was advised to watch what I was eating and perhaps limit the amount I ate.

It was the 1970s. Margarine was considered a healthy choice, and whilst my older sister was allowed access to as much bread with butter as she had the appetite for, I was limited to just one slice – with margarine.

The situation wasn't helped by my genuine fondness for food. The family story goes that my first few steps were taken, not in response to the endless encouragement, pleas and coaxing, but rather to get to some food from the table. With a hard lump of cheese in my hand, I then sat down, refusing to walk for another month or so.

Over time, a deepening struggle between my parents and me set in. When my dad left the kitchen, I would grab a slice of bread, stuffing it into my mouth. If there were biscuits and I got home from school first, I was straight over, climbing up the cabinets to get to the tin. My need for food, to get hold of it, to have as much as I could manage, became something that wasn't to do with my appetite. It became a tight, fast emotional reaction, using up a great deal of focus. I was determined to find a way to be in control.

Of course, my parents were at a loss to know what to do. 'You know the chocolates weren't yours, Anne, why did you eat them?' I remember them saying. Or 'We're really worried about you eating so much. Is there something wrong?' Sometimes my mum would be upset. 'What's wrong with you? Why can't you just stop?' she'd ask.

When confronted, a child will very rarely be able to explain why he has done something. Rather, it can *intensify the feeling that something deep is wrong. At that time, I was very aware that my behaviours didn't make sense, that I was different. Slowly, 'different' came to mean weaker, less trustworthy, deceitful and greedy. I couldn't understand my emotions. Why was I so needy and grabbing around food? Why couldn't I be unaffected like my big sister? It began to wear on my confidence and trust in myself.*

When a child comes to see his behaviour as bad, as upsetting to others and as out of control, shame and confusion begin to creep in. Shame is the most difficult emotion to work through. Shame affects a child's self-identity. It threatens both his sense of being okay and then, through this, his connection to others. The shame alienates a child from others, but also from himself. He might find it hard to think about the situation, he pulls away from conversations, he feels uncomfortable and exposed and lost. And so the intensity of the emotion builds up like the layers of an onion. The more lost and worried he feels about his emotional reactions, the more he avoids thinking about them. He pushes them away but they are stronger and keep triggering those same responses.

THE BENEFITS OF CONTAINING EMOTIONS

So far, I've given examples of situations where there was a significantly strong, stuck emotional response, but no matter the strength of the difficulty, every child struggles at some point with tight, reactive emotions. Sometimes these are obvious and loud; at other times they are more hidden but still dominating and problematic.

Left unchecked, tight, strong emotions can affect a child's concentration, motivation and confidence. They compel him to act out, to take control and react without fully understanding the consequences. Although these big emotions can feel both exciting and unnerving at the same time, they knock a child off balance and end up feeling overwhelming and heavy. The difficulty is that although a child can't manage these emotions without help, his reactions push others away and create a wall of shame and defensiveness.

When a child's behaviour is pushing others away or causing damage and distress, he needs his parents to steady the emotions and stop the damaging or dangerous behaviour. The process of steadying and orientating these emotional reactions is referred to as 'containing'. Containing emotions happens when an adult responds to these challenging emotions, placing limits on behaviours but reaching out and connecting with the vulnerable, fearful emotions that stand behind these reactions.

A parent who works to contain a child's emotions:

- Provides the child with a sense of safety and security
- Places limits on potentially damaging behaviour without making a child fearful or ashamed or impacting on his confidence
- Helps a child tune into the quieter, more vulnerable background emotions so that he can express himself and become more orientated and comfortable

Contained emotions no longer weigh a child down. He feels more able to regulate and manage without having to jump in and control anything that triggers them. He can begin to experience the emotion without having to act on it.

Importantly, containing emotions *doesn't* mean boxing feelings in, preventing them, or shoving them down. Rather, it means reducing fear and stopping a child from rushing in with harmful, difficult behaviours. When fear and the subsequent need for control are taken care of, the more vulnerable and confused emotions underneath get expressed, listened to, and thought about.

LEARNING TO RIDE THE EMOTIONAL BIKE

When I am explaining this process of containing a child's big emotions, I often use the example of learning to ride a bike.

In order to ride a bike, the two things a child needs to practise are steering and braking. If he can't steer the bike, he can't go anywhere, he just goes around in wobbly circles. Equally, if he can't put on the brakes, he gets pulled along by the bike and can't stop or get off. Worse still, he feels out of control and might find himself crashing into a passer-by.

At first, you are on hand to help him. You might hold the handlebars and keep the bike steady whilst he gets comfortable. Gradually, you give him more control, but if he looks like he's going to crash into someone or something, you slow him down and steer the bike away. Your job is to keep him safe so that he can learn the basic skills.

As time passes, your child gets more capable and can steady himself, steer and brake. Sensing this, you step back a bit. If he *does* lose control, you are on hand to help him reorientate and steady himself, supporting him until he re-finds his balance.

The great thing is that as a child gets older and more confident, he has the ability to use his bike to take him to interesting new places. He can decide where he wants to go, and the extra speed provided by the bike is really useful.

Can you see the link between this process and helping a child develop a sense of security and skilfulness around strong emotions? A child needs the ability to slow down and steer his emotions in order to interact and relate to his world and the people around him. The important thing with emotions is that you are there to keep him safe and help him direct his energy and focus, to help him learn when he needs strong, forceful emotions and when to let them calm down.

WHY CONTAINING AND CONNECTING TO BIG EMOTIONS IS GOOD FOR A CHILD'S EQ

Being able to move through tight, defensive emotions but also being able to connect to a supportive adult is an important foundation for emotional intelligence.

When you step in to limit a child's behaviour but nonetheless remain open emotionally, your child's emotions become orientated and fearfulness settles. The shame and confusion he feels around his behaviour shifts and moves away. His confidence in relationships increases and his emotions slow down.

With these big responses held and supported, your child:

- Feels more capable and comfortable around emotions
- Becomes more able to talk and reflect on emotions. Even when they feel difficult and uncomfortable, he keeps trying to explain and put words to his experiences.
- Is confident that he can reach out to you when big emotions do come, and that you can help slow them down and keep him safe
- Is able to gradually manage some of these big emotions himself without feeling out of control or needing to impose control on the outside world
- Comes to recognize what he really wants as opposed to what he feels compelled to do in the midst of strong emotions
- Is able to use his strong emotions to respond quickly and get things done, but he can also calm these down and bring in quieter, slower, more vulnerable emotions when he needs to
- Is less controlling and defensive around others. His strong emotions aren't a barrier to building up warm, open friendships.

HOW TO CONTAIN AND SOOTHE EMOTIONS

When adults contain children's emotions, they step away from energetically arguing or imposing control in an aggressive way and instead they are consistent. They slow things down. They think.

My friend's great grandmother, Nogga, embodied this perfectly.

Nogga was about 80 years old. I remember her being small but wide with big feet and big hands. We loved Nogga a great deal.

Nogga was not a person to rush around, she wasn't exciting or fun and she wouldn't have had the energy to drag us apart should we start fighting or being physically disruptive. She didn't have a big, deep, booming voice (rather, it was thin and wispy with a thick Hungarian accent). But she did have some particularly special talents: she was patient, consistent and loving, and she took a non-complicated interest in our wellbeing. Her presence in my friend's family provided a great anchor of stability and safety.

Nogga was good at matching her responses to the situation. She always created a sense of calm and space for reflection.

On one occasion when the boys kicked a football at the postman, she sent for them. The two big boys came in angry, cross and defensive.

Nogga assessed the boys as they came in. 'Well now, I think you're both too hot just at the moment and we won't be able to talk,' she told them. 'We need to give this a bit of time to settle and then we can work things out. But until then, I want you to give me the ball.' Ignoring the complaints and criticism, Nogga patiently waited for the ball to be handed over.

When we had had lunch and tidied away, Nogga sat the big boys down at the table and talked to them patiently and calmly. 'Now Mr Dean is an old friend of ours (conveying values), it cannot happen that we do this. Let us think, how we can make this right?'

Nogga patiently waited for the boys to come up with a few suggestions. 'Hmm,' she said, sitting back. 'And maybe we also make him a cake, yes?'

Nogga's approach was not complicated. She didn't analyse behaviour or dole out consequences, other than when she felt this was necessary to keep us safe or to repair injuries. Nogga was an old woman, so her approach definitely wasn't based on dominating us or energetically managing our behaviour. Rather, we children trusted her and (albeit begrudgingly) took ourselves to her when we had crossed a line.

FIND YOUR 'TRUE NORTH'

When I think about Nogga's approach to strong emotions, there are a few things that stand out for me:

- We felt safe with her.
- She gave herself time to think. This meant that her focus was steady and consistent. Her decisions had weight because they were thought through.
- She didn't become involved in repetitive arguments, but nor did she dismiss our feelings. If someone was still upset later, she made great effort to listen and accommodate their experiences.
- Rather than dwelling on the wrongness of the child or his behaviour, her focus was always on how things could be repaired and sorted out.

- When the emotional heat had died down, she helped us to think about righting wrongs and soothing hurts. The value she placed on others, their feelings and needs shone through. She made us feel part of this strong value base.

Our emotions give us direction. Nogga's emotions embodied a sense of what Kim John Payne, in his book *The Soul of Discipline*, would describe as 'True North'. She had a very stable, grounded sense of what was important. Her focus was on a child's wider needs, to feel safe and secure, to be connected to others.

When a child is fearful, defensive and insecure, his North becomes what Kim John Payne calls a 'Magnetic North'. He is pushed and pulled around by fleeting, changeable impulses. For example, the impulse to try and feel steady by controlling others, to feel powerful by taking things or damaging another's belongings, to feel important by insisting on his own preferences and choices. Magnetic North feels like an appealing direction, but it is short term and harmful. It is forever changing and shifting and can leave a child adrift.

Your job as a parent is to hold on to a stronger sense of True North. Your child's emotions might be strong and disorientated and pulling him towards Magnetic North, but if you remain steady and grounded, keeping a focus on the important things, all other things fall into place: Your child's emotions are more easily contained and settled. His reactions are calmer and steadier.

Having a sense of True North as a parent isn't a character trait and it doesn't have to come through years of experience. With steady practice it becomes a more habitual guide. Here are some steps to help you, the parent, ground yourself and strengthen your True North:

Allow Yourself Time
The pressures on parents can be intense and unending. There are 61 things you have to get done before lunch, you haven't

had time to read with your daughter (even though her teacher asked), the house is in a state, no one has fed the cat and now your son is getting wilder and wilder, throwing things at his sister and refusing to tidy up. Feeling overwhelmed, you try to impose immediate control over things. You just want it all to stop.

You are not alone in this experience. The job of parenting is demanding and tough. Emotions under pressure push for tight, defensive responses. You might find yourself thinking: *'I can't do this.'* *'He thinks he's in charge and I won't take it.'* *'He is... (controlling, spoilt, a nightmare).'*

Finally, there are the emotional hooks which pull parents into battle. When I say this, I have a visual picture of a big fishhook, dragging someone along. Your hook might be your child damaging something or swearing. Or it could be the littler things – him giggling, sticking his tongue out, mimicking, sneering or ignoring you. When you are hooked in, your emotions get stronger and more intense. You want to demand that your child stops that behaviour. You want to show him that you're in charge. The sense of struggle steps up a notch.

Through allowing yourself *time* to acknowledge these thoughts, feelings and hooks, you allow yourself time to process the situation. You compassionately recognize the stress and pressure you are under and you also see that your child is desperately trying to find control and feel strong.

When you take this time to notice that both you and your child are caught up with the same needs (to feel steady and capable) then you recognize that at that very moment, things are simple. Your child needs to be safe and those around him need to be safe. All the other things can take their turn in an orderly queue.

Look Beyond the Difficult and Challenging

A child's big, strong reactions hide confusion and vulnerability. Responding to these hidden needs, even though your child is behaving in a defensive and challenging way, helps these to surface (to be expressed). He understands that it is safe to show these feelings and gets your support.

Let me give you an example:

You child might be shouting: 'I hate you. I don't care what you say. You're stupid.'

When you look beyond the defensive, tight emotions, you know that underneath, he is upset and wounded, and you remind yourself to respond to these deeper needs.

You might say, 'It looks like you're feeling really frustrated and cross and you want me to know.' He might shout something more or say things to push you away but it's important you persist so he knows you mean it. You say: 'Let me come over to you so I can hear about it.'

Now, quite often it takes a child a while to relax and talk more openly, but that's okay. He notices that you're not arguing or getting defensive and he feels a change in you.

Initially he might refuse, and grumble. That's completely normal, his guard is up. But you're not arguing or getting defensive, and he'll feel the change in emotional tone. Slowly, he will feel less charged up. His voice will get lower and quieter. He might let you put a hand on his shoulder or give him a cuddle. Perhaps he'll tell you a bit more. The important thing is that he's no longer having to behave quite so powerfully and impulsively. He can allow himself to be more open and more vulnerable.

Find Your Confidence

A parent once commented to me that he didn't know what he would do when his children finally found out that really, he had no way of making them do anything. He was right. Ultimately, we don't have a magical way of controlling a child, of imposing our will over theirs. Thank goodness. The very essence of having a child with his own life and emotions is that, rather than being forcefully controlled, he is constantly learning and being guided alongside us.

But his comment spoke to something essential. It is important that parents find their confidence in these challenging moments. Emotions are quickly passed on, and children are very sensitive to how confident and sure we are. They want to feel secure and anchored and they are looking to you.

What we lack in control, we make up for in commitment and love. When I reflect on this, two things make me feel secure and purposeful as a parent in tough situations.

- The first is that I am deeply committed to my children. I will not let them behave in ways that would cause them or others harm. I want them to be able to move through fear without building up problems or becoming ashamed and isolated. I want their emotions to settle and steady so that they can feel orientated, connecting to their lives and to others. This means that whilst they are unsafe and acting out, I am unswerving and determined.
- The second important thing is knowing that my children want and need for me to be clear, steady and comfortable. To hold that sense of True North and to be able to orientate their emotions and calm their behaviour. I think back to Otto and how not having a consistent adult to do this placed such a considerable burden on him. I remember how he would come to me, rather than to the more relaxed playworker, because he wanted and needed help to manage these big, tiring emotions, even though my responses at the time were far from perfect.

The funny thing is that when you are secure and confident in *why* you are stepping in, your child recognizes your commitment and his emotions begin to slow and calm before you have even started thinking about what needs to be done.

STOP DISRUPTIVE BEHAVIOURS

A child's strong, tight, fast emotional reactions can feel as powerful as a storm. When the storm is whipping through, pushing over trees, fences and cars then it can be frightening and destructive. Your job as a parent is to bring the storm in and ground it safely. You help emotions to slow down whilst stopping behaviours which are harmful or damaging.

When a child is triggered and overwhelmed, he can lack the capacity to stop harmful or damaging behaviours himself and so we step in to protect and contain things. By this I mean both protecting him from the emotional consequences of destructive behaviour (guilt, overwhelm, damage to relationships), and also simply from being dominated by big, tight emotions. We are protecting him, not punishing him.

With the big, loud, aggressive behaviours, you step in clearly and with purpose: '*I am going to take those scissors away from you because I don't want anyone to get hurt.*' '*I'm stopping the car until you put your seat belt back on because you are not safe.*' '*I need you to come with me over here because you're frightening your brother.*' We know that our child is at risk if we don't stop his behaviour and so we are clear and sure and we persist.

There are also other more low-level behaviours that are less storm-like but can continue to rumble under the surface. Examples of these might be when a child is:

- Being constantly snappy
- Repetitively teasing his sibling
- Compulsively taking things
- Routinely refusing to do things such as showering or turning off screens

Knowing how to respond to the low-level yet persistent behaviours can paradoxically be harder than the big stormy behaviours. You are clear that you need to step in and stop obviously damaging and harmful behaviours but feel worn down by smaller behaviours such as teasing or refusing to do things. You don't want to escalate the situation, and anyway, you wonder whether you're overreacting as the behaviour often just passes.

Unfortunately, lower-level behaviours take up a lot of a child's emotional space, they are unsettling and they tend to slowly escalate. Most importantly, they're a sign that your child is struggling. In these situations, it's best to focus on just a couple of types of behaviours at any one time. These could be behaviours that are becoming more frequent or that are particularly upsetting for family members. This limited range stops you having to jump in over everything and gives focus and purpose. Most importantly, it recognizes that intervening isn't a negative thing. It isn't a punishment. Rather, the intent to help a child stop problematic behaviours is deeply caring and important for a child. It helps him to settle and resolve difficult emotions in more grounded, orientated ways.

Let me give you some examples of how you might contain lower-level but persistent behaviours:

Put a Buffer on Behaviour

If he's teasing or snapping at others, bring him to you. Start by acknowledging the emotion: *'You don't seem to be yourself; what's wrong?'*

Depending on how tense he is, this might be enough. But it can also be helpful to put a 'buffer' on the behaviour. By this I mean keeping your child near to you (kindly) so that he has a break from the other child and has a bit of care and attention from you.

Help Him Through

If your child refuses to do things (such as taking a shower) then you can help contain his emotions by coming in closer and helping him. You might say, '*I can see you're feeling fed up and cross. We need to make sure you have a shower. I'm going to come up with you. I'll turn it on and get the towel out and then when we're done we can come down and make some hot chocolate.*'

Persist Without Getting into a Struggle

The key things that create struggle are:

1. Arguments about whether a behaviour needs to stop
2. A parent not being persistent

When you need a child to stop a consistently disruptive behaviour:

- Don't try to reason with your child. It often simply distracts from what needs to happen. You can listen to and acknowledge a child's feelings but your main focus is on stopping the behaviour. When things have calmed down, you'll have more space to reflect and think with your child.
- If your child refuses to do something, such as give you the iPad when you've asked, then you need to give this your total focus. You stand near him, and matter-of-factly insist. He might start arguing or reasoning with you. This isn't the time for negotiations. You keep your focus on him giving you the iPad. Steady yourself, keep kind but firm and tell him that you need it. You can be low key and calm, but don't lose focus or change tack.
- Your child might shove the iPad at you, and storm off. This is fine. Give him a bit of time (say five minutes) and then

find him to see if he's okay. At this point his emotions will still be hot so your intention is to listen and help him to slow down and express himself if he feels okay with this.

MAKE SPACE FOR CONVERSATIONS ABOUT EMOTIONS

When we think about setting limits and keeping a child safe, it's important to be clear about the difference between the loud, fast emotions a child naturally experiences and the behaviours that can cause damage.

A child's strong emotions may be loud and forceful and very upset but safe. They are your child's internal experiences expressed in loud words, sobs, shaking and crying. These need to be recognized and acknowledged.

If, however, he's acting on the big emotions in a way that is unsafe or that blocks him reaching out or connecting to you, then this behaviour needs clear boundaries and limits. Without these limits, talking and connecting can't happen.

After the Storm

We have spoken a lot in this chapter about what happens in the heat of the moment. About steadying ourselves as parents and intervening confidently to stop harm. However, the real work happens afterwards – when the heated emotions have died down, when your child feels less threatened and more receptive. This is the time to fully acknowledge his emotions and help him feel more orientated.

The focus for these conversations is to allow a child's quieter emotions some space, to help him express any hurt and think about what happened. All of this allows him to feel safe, heard and secure. Children learn best when they are allowed to think openly and are supported, so your job is to try and fully understand his point of view rather than to challenge or quiz him.

Acknowledge Your Child's Emotions and Gently Explain Your 'True North'

It's important to remember that these conversations aren't about blame. If your child tells you that he thinks his behaviour was all your fault because you won't let him continue to play his computer game, then you might feel provoked into arguing your side. This is understandable but counterproductive as he will simply argue back. Rather, your job is to try and allow him to think things through himself. You try to get him to reflect on his feelings. You ask, *'What was the most difficult thing for you?'*

He might have felt disappointment, anger, frustration, envy at others he imagines are allowed to play with computers more. Whatever he says, your job is to try and open out his point so that he lets go of his isolation and sense of battle rather than getting caught in argument.

These conversations aren't completely one-way. When you have heard him out you can then say something about your perception of things. I do this once I have fully heard him out and validated his experience. Your child really won't be able to take on too much of your perspective, but if you keep it steady, clear and simple it helps him to reorientate.

I say things such as, *'I can see how much you love playing X game. They are so fun and fast-moving. One of the things that is also important to me is that it doesn't cause a lot of upset and arguments between us when your time is up.'* If he comes back again with his original position then let this be. Over time, he will come to see the your position much more effectively through your behaviour than through an argument.

ENCOURAGE RESPONSIBILITY

As children grow, their own sense of competence also extends – and they'll want to make you aware.

It was 10.20pm and I was going to bed. My eight-year-old son's light was on. I told him that the next night there would not be a light. That if I couldn't trust him to turn his light off by 8.30pm (like his sister) then I would take the light away the second night.

His face crumpled. 'I can decide things,' he said in a voice that wobbled slightly. 'I can decide when I want to read and when I want to sleep.'

I thought about it that night. His small but heartfelt response left me feeling unsettled. Of course I could control his behaviour, I could take away privileges, but his sense of himself, his confidence, also felt important.

The next morning, I said, 'How about we make a deal? I will come in and say, "lights out" at 8.30pm. If I forget then I can't tell you that your light should have been off or take it away. But if I do remind you and you keep reading, then it does?'

'I think that's a good idea, Mama,' he said.

I could tell for the rest of the morning he was happier. He was more communicative, open, chatty and connected to me.

A few nights later I had lost track of time again and hadn't gone up to remind him that his light should be out. By 8.45pm, he came downstairs. 'Mummy, I have had to do the remembering tonight,' he said sternly.

As parents do the work of containing a child's emotions and working through difficulties, children begin to internalize the process. They know the rules, the order of things and what is expected of them. They also have a desire to build up their own sense of natural control; to develop their confidence and sense of capability. It's therefore important that we help them along with this.

Normally I start small, beginning with everyday, not-too-hot situations and then I work with the child to think about how he builds up his skills. These everyday skills might be linked to managing small amounts of tight emotions or situations where children have to contain relatively low-level disruptive behaviours such as getting ready for walks without moaning, tidying up all together (without the typical culprit not joining in and creating problems), remembering not to automatically moan before you've even tried dinner (a big one in our family).

When picking an area, beware of trying to help a child manage emotions around screen time or computer games. It might look like a relatively good area to try and reduce arguments, but screens can be very all-consuming and mostly it's better just to have very clear boundaries around finish times rather than trying to negotiate or vary these or relying too much on a child's own orientation.

Following Nogga's example, I try my best to talk to children collaboratively. Nogga used 'we' a lot when she spoke to us. She would make suggestions then patiently listen to our thoughts. She was always ready for grown-up conversations: 'What should we do? What's the best way to sort this out?' she would ask.

Children love it when their expertise and advice is asked for. It makes them feel competent and included and it keeps shame away. I often begin 'What about if...'. I also tend to offer something myself first and then the child (picking up on this give-and-take) responds back with something. In the example of my son and his light, I pledged to take responsibility for reminding him and he, in turn would take responsibility for keeping the light off. When conversations are easy and spacious, it gives the child time to warm up to ideas and think from a more grown-up perspective.

As children get used to this process, they can become master negotiators. This is certainly true for my eldest son. I'll explain a problem and he tends to like to think of a reward system for it. As long as this is set up in a truly collaborative manner and as long as I think I'm getting a good deal, I have no problem with this. So he'll come up with a (hopefully) not-too-outlandish suggestion. I'll say, *'Okay but this is to help you learn how to tidy up your bedroom in the morning without moaning, this is not a long-term thing.'* My son will screw up one side of his face trying to wink. *'Right y'are,'* he'll say and then we shake on it.

The reward might be something like crumble and custard for pudding, or five minutes more play before bedtime, but the overall outcome is positive. My son feels like his agency and autonomy is being respected, he practises doing something which is relatively simple, and it quickly becomes a habit. And rather than feeling that he is only doing it for the reward (as some people worry will happen with these rewards systems), when he is involved from the outset, he feels competent and grown-up using his new habit and it tends to stick around.

Of course, the deal is always open to further discussion. The child agrees not to moan about something, but if they have constructive suggestions (ie different walks, alternative meal ideas) then they can come to me about this later.

5 POINTS TO REMEMBER FROM STEP 5

- **When you contain and connect to your child's difficult emotions your focus is on strengthening your emotional connection to your child.** You recognize that the challenging, defensive behaviours you can see are driven by fear and anxiety. Rather than getting caught up in a struggle with these difficult behaviours, you put clear limits on these so that you can connect to the more vulnerable underlying emotions.

- **Containing emotions doesn't mean boxing emotions in, preventing them or shoving them down.** It means slowing down the controlling or problematic reactions so that you can help your child work through the emotions underlying these behaviours.

- **Your child's strong, controlling reactions hide disorientated, vulnerable emotions.** When you are steady and grounded and respond to his hidden need to feel safe and orientated, he stops trying to battle through situations on his own. He tunes in to you and your guidance, and feels safer sharing his fears and worries with you.

- **Containing a child's big, defensive emotions can be hard on parents.** A child's emotions can trigger quick, strong feelings of anger and panic in parents along with the impulse to control back. By compassionately recognizing the stress and pressure you are experiencing, you give yourself time to process the situation. You let go of unhelpful ideas around blame and guilt; and instead focus on doing what you can to step away from struggles, limit disruptive behaviour and connect with your child.

- **When you repeatedly limit problematic behaviours and connect to the more vulnerable feelings, your child begins to slow down his reactions.** He can reflect on the times when he feels tight and stuck and can join with you to problem solve around areas of repetitive difficulty.

FINAL WORDS

Developing Emotional Ease and Connection

Much can be said about the sheer hectic busyness of modern parenting. The struggle to keep your child physically safe and healthy, to get through the washing, meals, childhood illnesses, birthday parties as well as the pressure to help her academically and socially. But throughout all of this busyness, the true task of parenting happens around emotions.

For whilst you and your child are moving through the days, learning to tie shoelaces and check carefully before crossing the road, her emotions are facing their own unique and sometimes hard-to-fathom, developmental mountain – and you are her guide.

The challenges your child experiences on her way up this mountain are very particular and often take a great deal of resourcefulness. As she is climbing, she leans on you. For both of you this can be tiring work. She needs your capability and understanding but you can't always see her mountain or understand what it is she is trying to navigate. She might be working out how she can come to be more confident in friendships whilst simultaneously facing down an assortment of doubts and uncertainties. You do your best, but trying to help her can be confusing and sometimes bewildering.

As a parent you look for reassurance that your child is learning and developing, but the emotional mountain your child is climbing – with all its encounters and trials – means she often isn't focusing on the emotional tasks you or I might have in mind, such as honesty or kindness or empathy. Instead, she's trying to cope with the many confusing emotions jumping around as she attempts to get on with other things. She wants to be more decisive and stronger, which means working out what to do with all the anxious, timid feelings around. She would love to look cool socially and to make others like her and so, just for today, she mustn't be dragged back by unease around the friend who's been left out.

On many levels, your child wants to make you proud, but the mountain she is climbing is very demanding. She tries to push and pull her emotions around but the 'determined' ones become strained and exhausted, whilst the 'vulnerable' emotions become intense and noisy. Often, she feels disorientated, rudderless and stuck.

This is where your persistence and belief come in. Whilst her emotional intelligence is so new and inexperienced, your job is to be around so that you can lend her yours. You step in to calm and slow things down. Rather than glossing over her struggles, dismissing her priorities or deciding what she should care about (another mountain in itself), you move in to understand. You work hard to see her dilemmas and her difficulties on *her* mountain.

When you're helping your child deal with this emotional journey, things can be bumpy and demanding. Sometimes, your child's behaviours are difficult and provoking. You get tired, frustrated, and are often worried. Not only are you helping her to grow stronger emotionally, so too are you having to regulate your own emotions. To work through your own understandings. To settle your own doubts and worry.

There will be many times when she seems to be pushing you away, but with effort and compassion, you look beyond her defensiveness and see her need for emotional connection.

And because you have the capacity to see through the different fears and confusions that arise, you help her to find less-constricted, more-nuanced emotions, and both of you develop and grow.

Slowly you notice that the emotions that had seemed so jarring and difficult don't seem to be so very bad or disruptive.

The vulnerable, apprehensive emotions that you worried would overwhelm her have instead helped her find support and actually strengthened her confidence and independence. She is finding her own pace and timing for repairs: the guilt and unease she has been quietly feeling over the excluded friend has its moment. It motivates her to find a way to bring that person back into the group. Her emotions seem to be working through their challenges in their own way. Things don't fall apart.

All of this quiet development happens in its own particular, quirky way. Through her relationship with you, she finds many more ways to be human and to respond. So rather than swapping out her shouty, expressive, reactive emotions for serenity and reflection, you help her to become more agile. Where before she was tense and alert, with you by her side, she is tense and alert *and* humorous. Maybe she adds some of her own mock-sophisticated superiority and then, steadied by your acceptance and love, she adds curiosity and kindness.

These emotional shifts and developments happen through your relationship with her. You help her to deal with fears and to slow down the fast, loud emotions. You are open and receptive to the many ways in which she is learning. Rather than seeing emotional intelligence as a place she will get to, you tune into her experiences more and all the small, incremental emotional tasks she is navigating, slowing down your reactions to help her adapt and develop.

And because of you, her worry shifts and enjoyment and learning take centre stage. Through your eyes, she understands that her efforts and hopes are important. It's a very good emotional beginning.

ACKNOWLEDGEMENTS

Thanks to my editor, Beth Bishop, whose perceptive comments and suggestions really helped me to make sense of this book and bring it to life. It's been such a pleasure to collaborate with you.

Thanks to my agent, Maddy Belton from Graham Maw Christie Agency. Her support was invaluable, particularly in the midst of the COVID-19 lockdown when the idea of writing a coherent sentence, let alone a book, seemed a million miles away.

Special thanks to my sister-in-law and close friends for all of their kind, 'emergency' childcare. And also to the same lovely sister-in-law for the sane advice and words of encouragement when I really needed them.

Finally, thanks to my family who have put up with being repeatedly referred to in this book as the only undisguised case studies. And, of course, to Crispin for his steady support and frequent picking-up of the pieces.

REFERENCES

Burkeman, O (2020). The Eight Secrets to a Fairly Fulfilled Life. *Guardian [online]*. *Available at* www.theguardian.com/lifeandstyle/2020/sep/04/oliver-burkemans-last-column-the-eight-secrets-to-a-fairly-fulfilled-life

Cohen, L (2012). *Playful Parenting: An Exciting New Approach to Raising Children that will Help you Nurture Close Connections, Solve Behavior Problems and Encourage Confidence*. Ballantine Books.

Faber, A and Mazlish, E (2012). *How to Talk so Kids Will Listen and Listen so Kids Will Talk*. Piccadilly Press.

Greenspan, S (1998). *The Growth of The Mind: And the Endangered Origins of Intelligence*. Da Capo Press.

Lindsey, EW, and Mizem, J (2000). Parent–child physical and pretend play: Links to children's social competence. Merrill-Palmer Q J Dev Psychol, 46, pp. 565–591.

Payne, KJ (2015). *The Soul of Discipline: The Simplicity Parenting Approach to Warm, Firm and Calm Guidance – From Toddler to Teens*. Ballantine Books Inc.

Robbins, T (1980). *Still Life with a Woodpecker*. Bantam Books.

Schore, A (2015). *Early Right Brain Regulation and the Relational Origins of Emotional Well-Being*. Children Australia.

Winnicott, DW (2016). *The 'Good-enough Mother' [Radio broadcast]*. Available at blog.oup.com/2016/12/winnicott-radio-broadcasts

Winnicott, DW (1990). *Home is Where We Start From: Essays by a Psychoanalyst*. Penguin.

USEFUL RESOURCES

UK
Action for Children: www.parents.actionforchildren.org.uk
Bridge the Gap Emotional Education: www.jwbridgethegap.com
Care for the Family: www.careforthefamily.org.uk
Emotion Works: www.emotionworks.org.uk
Family Lives: www.familylives.org.uk
Kidscape: www.kidscape.org.uk
MindEd Hub: www.minded.org.uk
Wee Seeds: www.weeseeds.co.uk
Young Minds: www.youngminds.org.uk

EUROPE
The Alliance for Childhood European Network Group:
www.allianceforchildhood.eu
ChildHub: childhub.org

USA
Child Mind Institute: childmind.org
Committee for Children: www.cfchildren.org
Very Well Family: www.verywellfamily.com

CANADA
Caring for Kids: www.caringforkids.cps.ca

AUSTRALIA AND NEW ZEALAND
Beyond Blue Health Families: healthyfamilies.beyondblue.org.au
Kids Helpline (for young people aged between 5 and 25 years):
www.kidshelpline.com.au
ReachOut: www.about.au.reachout.com

NOTES

ABOUT US

Welbeck Balance publishes books dedicated to changing lives. Our mission is to deliver life-enhancing books to help improve your wellbeing so that you can live your life with greater clarity and meaning, wherever you are on life's journey. Our Trigger books are specifically devoted to opening up conversations about mental health and wellbeing.

Welbeck Balance and Trigger are part of the Welbeck Publishing Group – a globally recognized independent publisher based in London. Welbeck are renowned for our innovative ideas, production values and developing long-lasting content. Our books have been translated into over 30 languages in more than 60 countries around the world.

If you love books, then join the club and sign up to our newsletter for exclusive offers, extracts, author interviews and more information.

www.welbeckpublishing.com   **www.triggerhub.org**

🐦 welbeckpublish   🐦 Triggercalm
📷 welbeckpublish   📷 Triggercalm
f welbeckuk   f Triggercalm